WASSERSTROM

D0752939

MANICHAEAN LITERATURE

UNESCO COLLECTION
OF REPRESENTATIVE WORKS

THE VOLUMES IN THE PERSIAN HERITAGE SERIES
ARE JOINTLY SPONSORED BY UNESCO
AND THE PAHLAVI FOUNDATION'S ROYAL INSTITUTE
OF TRANSLATION AND PUBLICATION

Persian Heritage Series
No. 22
Ehsan Yar-Shater, General Editor

MANICHAEAN LITERATURE

*Representative Texts Chiefly from
Middle Persian and Parthian Writings*

Selected, introduced, and partly translated by

Jes P. Asmussen

SCHOLARS' FACSIMILES & REPRINTS
Delmar, New York
1975

First published in 1975 by
Scholars' Facsimiles & Reprints, Inc.,
P.O. Box 344, Delmar, New York 12054

© 1975 Scholars' Facsimiles & Reprints, Inc.

Library of Congress Cataloging in Publication Data

Asmussen, Jes Peter, comp.
    Manichaean literature.
    (UNESCO collection of representative works, Persian series)   (Royal
Institute for Translation and Publication of Iran, Persian Heritage series; no. 22)
    Bibliography: p.
    Includes index.
    1. Manichaeism — History — Sources. I. Title. II. Series: III. Series:
UNESCO collection of representative works, Persian series.
BT1410.A72   273'.2   74-22063
ISBN 0-8201-1141-4

PERSIAN HERITAGE SERIES

EDITOR
EHSAN YAR-SHATER *(Columbia University)*

ADVISORY COUNCIL
I. GERSHEVITCH *(University of Cambridge)*
G. LAZARD *(University of Paris)*
G. MORGENSTIERNE *(University of Oslo)*
B. SPULER *(University of Hamburg)*
G. TUCCI *(University of Rome)*
T.C. YOUNG *(Princeton University)*

LATE MEMBERS
A.J. ARBERRY *(University of Cambridge)*
W.B. HENNING *(University of California, Berkeley)*
H. MASSÉ *(University of Paris)*

The *Persian Heritage Series* is published under the
joint auspices of UNESCO and the Pahlavi Foundation's
Royal Institute of Translation and Publication. It is the aim
of this series to make available the outstanding works of
Persian authors in the various fields of the humanities and
the sciences. The translations in the series are intended
not only to satisfy the needs of the students of Persian history
and culture, but also to respond to the demands of the
intelligent reader who seeks to broaden his intellectual and
artistic horizons through an acquaintance with major world
literatures.

Volumes published in the Persian Heritage Series

IN ENGLISH

FERDOWSI, *The Epic of the Kings*, tr. R. Levy
ATTAR, *Muslim Saints and Mystics*, tr. A.J. Arberry
RUMI, *Mystical Poems I*, tr. A.J. Arberry
TANSAR, *The Letter of Tansar*, tr. M. Boyce
TUSI, *The Nasirean Ethics*, tr. G.M. Wickens
VARAVINI, *Tales of Marzuban*, tr. R. Levy
RASHID AL-DIN, *The Successors of Genghis Khan*, tr. J.A. Boyle
MOHAMMAD IBN IBRAHIM, *The Ship of Sulaiman*, tr. J. O'Kane
GORGANI, *Vis o Ramin*, tr. G. Morrison
AVICENNA, *The Metaphysica of Avicenna (ibn Sina)*, tr. P. Morewedge
FASAI, *History of Persia Under the Qajar Rule*, tr. H. Busse
BIGHAMI, *Love and War*, tr. W. Hanaway, Jr.
F. HEKMAT, *Folk Tales of Ancient Persia*

IN FRENCH

NIZAMI, *Chosroes et Chirine*, tr. H. Masse
ARUZI, *Les Quatre Discours*, tr. I. de Gastine
FARAMARZ, *Samak-e Ayyar*, tr. F. Razvani
ATURPAT-I EMETAN, *Denkart III*, tr. Jean de Menasce

IN ITALIAN

NEZAMI, *Le Sette Principesse*, tr. A. Bausani

IN GERMAN

RUMI, *Licht und Reigen*, tr. J. Ch. Bürgel

IN THE PRESS

SAADI, *Bustan*, tr. G. M. Wickens
ANON., *The History of Sistan*, tr. M. Gold
KHAYYAM, *The Rubaiyat*, tr. P. Kasra
ANON., *Le Livre d'Ardaviraz*, tr. Ph. Gignoux
ANON., *Le Livre de Sendbade*, tr. D. Bogdanovitch
NISHAPURI, *The History of the Saljuqs* tr. K. A. Luther
ESKANDAR BEG MONSHI, *The History of Shah Abbas the Great*, tr. R. M. Savory

All inquiries about the Persian Heritage Series should be directed to The Iran Center, 602 Kent Hall, Columbia University, New York, N. Y. 10027.

Contents

Introduction

The doctrine of salvation established by the Persian *Mani* in the third century A.D.[1] was considered from the beginning as directly dangerous to the existing religious communities. Both Christian and Zarathustrian were inflamed with hatred against this man and his teachings, which were soon widely extended by the strongly proselytizing Manichaean church. Kartir the *mobad*, whom the Manichaeans held directly responsible for Mani's tragic end, was particularly active among the Zarathustrians. In a great inscription, Kartir asserts with much self-satisfaction that during his lifetime the Manichaeans suffered heavy persecution in the Sasanian kingdom.[2] He was also represented in Manichaean literature as a man of evil design.[3] But Kartir was not alone in this respect. The Zarathustrian animosity against Manichaeism was sustained for centuries, and is particularly apparent in the great theological literature of the ninth century. For example, in *Shkand gumānīk vičār* ("The doubt-crushing explanation," *sc.* of Zoroastrianism in relation to Islam, Christianity, Jewry, and Manichaeism) all of chapter 16 is devoted to the clash with Mani and his heritage. The whole of *Gujastak Abālish* (The accursed Abalish) describes a disputation between the *zandik* Abalish and the *mobad* Aturfarnbag, with an outcome which, of course, as becomes apparent from the very first line, is tragic for Abalish who became completely paralyzed; indeed, "he was as if killed" (IX, 4).[4] In the equally important but obscure masterpiece *Dēnkart*, differences are set out under twelve headings between Manichaeism, here represented by Mani himself, and Zoroastrianism, represented by Aturpat-i Mahraspandan (ed. Madan 216.19-218.15). No opportunity was lost to show disgust towards Mani and his teaching.

In the West, Manichaeism was already a force at the end of the third century; it is mentioned in an edict of the Emperor *Diocletian* of 297,[5] a portent of its coming popularity in the Mediterranean provinces of the Roman Empire. And in about the year 300, the neo-platonist Alexander of Lycopolis in Upper Egypt wrote his famous treatise opposing the teachings of the Manichaeans,[6]

which are refuted point by point. This was the neo-platonists'
attack on gnosticism in the spirit of Plotin and Porphyrios.

The theologians of the ancient church were beginning to see
the danger, and the first great Christian anti-Manichaean work
now appeared. This was Hegemonius' *Acta Archelai*, which laid
down the general lines followed in subsequent centuries by the
stereotyped Christian polemic.[7] Afrem the Syrian devoted a very
large part of his extensive production to the struggle against Mani,
who is usually attacked together with Bardaisan and Marcion.
To Afrem, Mani was the devil's raiment, *mānā*, a play on the
phonetic similarity to the name Mani.[8] At almost the same time
as Afrem, Athanasius' friend, Serapion of Thmuis, wrote his
treatise opposing the Manichaeans, but without a very profound
knowledge of his subject.[9] His concern was not to give a detailed
exposition of Manichaean theology, but to refute it. The treatise
is therefore primarily an attack on dualism. Perhaps his main
intention was not in any way to clash with Manichaeism, but to
assert a not generally sanctioned dogma, the dogma of the absolute
goodness of human nature. If this is the case, he acknowledged his
inheritance from Anthonius, whose favorite disciple he was.[10]
A few years later, Bishop Titus of Bostra wrote four books in Greek
opposing the teachings of Mani,[11] provoked according to Photius
by the Manichaean apostle Addai. The original Greek text has
survived only fragmentarily, but a complete Syriac version has
been preserved.[12]

At the end of the century the young Augustine was won over
to Manichaeism, and for nine years he participated in the life of
the community as "Hearer." The thorough insight into and
understanding of Mani's teaching that he acquired during these
nine years later made him its most dangerous opponent. Augustine,
in many treatises, took his revenge on his earlier faith with great
passion and thoroughness. Even in those treatises not themselves
concerned with opposition to Manichaeism, sooner or later he
refers to it.[13] Almost the whole of Augustine's production is therefore a first-rate source of information about this religion.

During the subsequent centuries, anti-Manichaean writing
continued to increase, although original contributions were few.
However, Evodius' fifth-century treatise against the Manichaeans,

which is concerned with the Manichaean cosmogony with quotations from *Epistula Fundamenti*, should be mentioned.[14] But of course a systematic treatment of the sources available — true research — was not in evidence. An objective evaluation of Manichaeism was perhaps at that time a psychological impossibility. Manichaeism was too burning a question to be subjected to sober, impersonal description.

The first scholarly monograph on Manichaeism was the *Histoire critique de Manichée et du Manichéisme* by the Huguenot Isaac de Beausobre dating from the first half of the eighteenth century.[15] As a member of a persecuted minority, he doubtless had a certain sympathy for the universally disliked Manichaeans. Although of course this work does not completely satisfy the present day requirements for a scientific work, it is still of enormous value. Beausobre had in certain aspects a clearer insight than most later scholars into, for example, Mani's sources for the book on the fallen angels and their giant sons (cf. *Gen.* 6).[16]

The nineteenth century led Manchaean research into fruitful channels. The old material was subjected to new and profitable investigation, taking in previously unknown sources. This intense nineteenth century research activity was all the more welcome, since Central Asian finds at the beginning of the present century produced completely different and unforeseen problems.

F.C. Baur's *Das manichäische Religionssystem* appeared in 1831 and provided a very thorough and systematic treatment of the material available on the primitive church. The school of Tübingen's historical philosophy influenced the work, and Baur's general view in its extreme form — Manichaeism as an Indo-Buddhist system — is unacceptable. However, the scientific imagination and high degree of accuracy displayed by Baur in this work makes it a landmark in the history of research. Even when investigating the new finds in Chinese Turkestan, it was necessary to refer to it repeatedly.

New source material was added when Gustav Flügel published *Mani: Seine Lehre und seine Schriften* in 1862. This made Ibn an-Nadim's section on Manichaeism in *Kitab al-Fihrist*, "The Catalogue," accessible to scholars.[17] In this connection, it is of great importance that Ibn an-Nadim appears to have based his account extensively on genuine Manichaean writings. Al-Bīrūnī's refreshingly impartial account, published by Sachau in 1878, is incidentally of similar importance.[18] Kessler's book on Mani of 1889 appeared under the banner of pan-Babylonism;[19] this, in its analysis, took a closer look at *Acta Archelai* and the Syriac sources, and reached beautiful but not always equally tenable results. Towards the end of the century, the Syriac material was extended by an important source, the *Book of Scholia, Ketaba d'eskolyon*, by the Syrian Theodore bar Kōnai from the eighth century, published with a translation by the French consul in Aleppo, H. Pognon.[20]

Great documentary finds usually solve many problems and leave still more unsolved. This — as at present with the Qumran finds — also applies to the find of Manichaean manuscripts in Central Asia. The importance of these finds cannot however be over-estimated. One suddenly found oneself, as concerns Manichaeism, in possession of texts written by Manichaeans for Manichaeans, and moreover from areas where Manichaeism was the state-protected religion. One was no longer subjected exclusively to the more or less one-sided polemic of spiteful opponents. European expeditions brought home the finds, and when in 1904 the great German Orientalist F.W.K. Müller[21] led research along the correct philological paths the publication of one great text followed another — in Middle-Persian, Parthian, Sogdian, Chinese and Uighur — while at the same time original viewpoints broke new ground in the study of Manichaeism. A temporary zenith was reached with the publication of W.B. Henning's texts originating from the literary remains of the great German Iranologist, F.C. Andreas, "Mitteliranische Manichaica aus Chinesisch-Turkestan I-III" dating from the beginning of the 1930s.[22] A synthetizing and syncretic monograph on Manichaeism was published by H.C. Puech in 1949 (cf. note 7), and much valuable material and quite a number of fundamental studies have since been added, not least through W.B. Henning himself, but also, and in a prominent way, by his pupil Professor Mary Boyce and orientalists like O. Kliima[23] in Prague, Geo. Widengren[24] in Uppsala, and Peter Ziehme and Werner Sundermann in the German Democratic Republic. Still, however, many difficulties remain, although several were solved, when, in the beginning of the 1930s, greatly important genuine Manichaean texts suddenly were placed at the disposal of research: the Coptic codices from Egypt, in all probability Fayum, nine in all, containing six different writings, of which the so-called *Kephalaia*, "Main Points" (in Manichaean dogmatics), a *Psalm-Book*, and some *Homilies* have been published. Unfortunately important parts of this Coptic library were definitively lost during World War II. [25] But, happily, lacunas in our knowledge are then filled out through unexpected findings of new material. In the year of 1969 restorative work made possible the reading of a Greek parchment codex in the papyrus collection of Cologne, and a Mani biography of sensational character also was produced. [26] This text, presumably from the fifth century and from Oxyrhynchos in Egypt, is a manuscript en miniature (4.5 × 3.5 cm.) and bears the title *On the Genesis (génna) of his* (i.e., Mani) *Body*. It is a Greek translation of a Syriac original and thus a further testimony to the words of Mani (cf. p. 12) that his religion, in distinction to the previous ones, appears in *all* languages! [27]

I. Mani and his Religion: Texts and Studies

Manichaeism is among the wide-spread and immensely popular religious movements of ancient times that are generally summarized under the name of gnosticism. One of the most burning problems in religio-historical research in recent years has been the dating of these movements, a problem provoked not least by newly-discovered texts such as the Dead Sea scrolls. No definite answer has as yet been given, but everything seems to point to these movements having had their roots quite certainly in pre-Christian times, but not attaining their typical physiognomy until Christianity and its special concept of the heavenly redeemer — Jesus. As the word indicates (from the Greek *gnosis*, "knowledge, cognition"), gnosticism offered people a knowledge, only the full apprehension of which could bring to the soul, the true inner self, final redemption from the corruption and evil of this world and lead it back to the heavenly regions where, according to gnostic thought, it had its true and original home. The soul's hope of salvation, of redemption, was the one great concern; the longing for the wonderful, pure, divine World of Light. A beautiful general manifestation of gnostic piety is given by, for example, the so-called *Odes of Solomon*, here XXV:

1) I was rescued from my bonds;
   And unto thee, my God, I fled.
2) For thou wast the right hand of my salvation,
   And my helper.
3) Thou hast restrained them that rise up against me,
   And they were seen no more:
4) Because thy face was with me,
   Which saved me by thy grace.
5) But I was despised and rejected in the eyes of many,
   And I was in their eyes like lead;
6) And I acquired strength from thyself,
   And help.

7) Thou didst set me a lamp at my right hand and at my left,
   That in me there may be nothing that is not bright;
8) And I was covered with the covering of thy spirit;
   And I removed from me the raiment of skins.
9) For thy right hand lifted me up,
   And removed sickness from me.
10) And I became mighty in thy truth,
    And holy by thy righteousness;
11) And all my adversaries were afraid of me:
    And I became the Lord's by the name of the Lord:
12) And I was justified by His gentleness,
    And His rest is for ever and ever.

[Rendel Harris and Alphonse Mingana, *The Odes and Psalms of Solomon*, vol. 2, 1920, p. 346]

... This ode might well have been written by Mani!

Although these movements had a uniform basic structure, there were great differences in the ways and means employed in the attainment of gnosis, a wild libertinism in some systems contrasting with an almost frighteningly realistic attitude towards sin and salvation in others. Manichaeism falls under the latter category. Here, also gnosis, knowledge, was the prerequisite for salvation. Without knowledge, no salvation:

... what (is) totally mixed up with evil and temporal and limited and transient. And the wise and those by whom the (religious) law is decided are capable of recognizing the unbounded and timeless and unmixed goodness of paradise in the bounded and temporal and mixed goodness of the material world. And in the same way the incalculable and unbounded evil of hell is known to exist through the numerable and bounded evil that is seen in the material world. And if in the material world one did not see the bounded and transient goodness and evil and the mixture of one another, (then) the order to stay far away from evil and to come to goodness would not come to the thought of anybody.

And if the soul does not see the knowledge that (has come) to it through myriads of births, by the help of ... that to it not before ... (and does not see) the benefit that (comes) from recognizing the eternal and timeless and unmixed goodness, then it is in need of a companion and guide who shows it the way and the passage that (take it) to the salvation from evil and the coming to the soul, that is the eternal and unmixed and imperishable goodness. But let there not be anybody saying: "If the knowledge, however, cannot come to man except through the doors that I have described above, then these doors should be right and alike, as far as knowledge and similar things are concerned, for *any* dogma," then the answer in this matter is this: In many places in this book I have shown that the cause of (the strength of) the mixture that (comes) to it through its being sectarian (?), is (dependent on) how much and how little knowledge the soul has. And the one who thinks or says this, he in this...

[M 9 I, Middle Persian: *MM* II, pp. 297-99; *Cat.* p. 2, *BBB* p. 77]

Here, also, the salvation of the soul was its getting free of the body, its prison, from which it is radically different in substance and nature:

... And then, when both of these, the (purely) corporeal (part) as well as the spirit (of the body), both are dark and ignorant and injurious and of one nature and the being and the substance of the body, one must ask this: What is the substance and nature of the soul itself? And as the nature and substance of the soul has been explained in many places in this book, then there is no doubt connected with knowing this: the soul is in substance different from the body and is in the body so mixed and fashioned and bound with the spirit of the body, that is wrath and concupiscence and lust, like ... (outside the state) of being of the same substance the mixture and fashioning and binding cannot be so as (in the case of) pure silver in which, because it is one and unmixed, the existence of any mixture and fashioning and binding with its own kind is visible. But if the silver is mixed with copper or with any other (kind of metal), the mixture and fashioning and binding that it has with that (metal), whatever it is, will appear in it in the same way as (in) a cooper drachm or a counterfeit coin. And in exactly the very same way, like the silver in the copper, the soul (is bound) in the coarseness and corporeality of the body, that is bone and flesh and skin and blood and breath and ... and dirt, by the bond of the spirit (of the body).

[M 9 II, Middle Persian: *MM* II, pp. 299-300; *Cat.* p. 2]

Mani, the founder and organizer of this religion, was born on 14 April 216 (year 527 according to the Seleucid era) in the province of Babylon:

"I am a grateful pupil hailing from the land of Babel. I hail from the land of Babel, and I have been placed in the gate of truth. I am a singer, a pupil who was led out of the land of Babel. I was led out of the land of Babel in order to cry out a cry in the world. You, (oh) Gods, I implore, all you Gods, forgive me (my) sins through mercy."

[M 4, 2 V, Parthian: *HR* II, p. 51 f.; *Cat*. p. 2]

"I have come before the King! Peace upon you from the Gods!" The King said: "Whence are you?" I said: "I am a physician from the land of Babylon." ... and in the whole body the girl became healthy, (and in) great joy she said to me: "Whence are you, my God and Vivifier and my...."

[M 566 I, Parthian: *HR* II, p. 87; *Cat*. p. 40]

There is no fixed literary statement that Mani was a physician by profession, in the strict sense of the word, He was the physician of the souls, the "Healing King," as a Chinese text has it, just like Buddha and above all Jesus *(Christus medicus)*, who by his spiritual power also cured people physically.

Tradition has it that his mother was of noble (Arsacid) birth, and there is every reason to believe this tradition to be historically correct, since it was sustained even under the Sasanids who came to power a few years after Mani's birth and sought in every way to draw the veil of oblivion over their dethroned predescessors. His father, Patig, was deeply concerned with questions of religion, and belonged to a baptist movement, "those who practise ablutions" (Ibn an-Nadim), or "those who purify themselves" (Theodore bar Konai), who as their head, Ibn an-Nadim says, had al-Khasih, i.e., Elkhasaios, a statement hitherto considered impossible, but now, however, convincingly verified by the Greek *Mani Codex*, in which Mani calls him "the founder *(arkhegos)* of your Law" *(MC* p. 135). Mani vehemently protested against the baptisms and purifications and eating taboos held redeeming by this Jewish-Christian sect. To him they were just external things, a material purity and not the purity of the spirit that only the really redeeming gnosis imparts, the gnosis that "releases the soul from death and destruction" *(MC* pp. 137-38). But this heavy attack, according to Mani, was in the very spirit of Elkhasaios. *He* had understood Elkhasaios correctly! The followers of Elkhasaios, however, represented by the worldly minded presbyter Sita, were of quite a different opinion and arranged a synod: "Then Sita and the mul-

titude of his companions made a synod of presbyters for my sake.
They also called the house-master (i.e., presbyter) Pattikios (i.e.,
Patig, Mani's father) and said to him: Your son has turned away
from our Law and wants to go out into the world" (*MC* pp. 156-57).
They broke off relations, and Mani was excommunicated, but
his father and two other Elkhasaites followed him. The "Twin",
Mani's heavenly self, which communicated "officially" with him
on two occasions, the first when he was aged twelve (cf. Jesus
as the twelve-year-old in the Temple, *Luke* 2, 41 f.), and the second
when he was aged 24 gave him courage and encouragement:
"Come forth and wander about! For see, two men from that
Law (Religion) will come to you and be your followers. In the same
way also Pattikios will be the first one of your Election (i.e., Church)
and follow you" (*MC* pp. 130-31). This "Twin," which is equally
Mani himself, is identified in western Manichaeism with the Holy
Ghost of the Christians, and in eastern Manichaeism with Maitreya,
the messianic emissary of Buddhism. With the second revelation,
Mani's religious self-assurance matured. He was now *Mani Khayya*,
the "living Mani," the Mani who was a participator in the true
life and was able to pass on the redeeming knowledge of it. With
this added Syriac adjective, his name was Grecized into Manichaios,
and he became generally known in that form even in Central Asia.
Mani and his Twin, his "Higher Ego"

> "[I] said: 'You ... and from your hand ... and other things (?)
> you have given [and] brought to me.' And even now he himself
> accompanies me, and he himself keeps and protects me. And in
> his power I fight with Āz (i.e., Greed) and Ahrmēn (i.e., the
> devil) and teach men wisdom and knowledge and save them
> from Āz and Ahrmēn. And these affairs of the Gods and the
> wisdom and knowledge of the gathering of the souls (viz. for
> salvation) that I have received from the Twin, I ... through
> the Twin ... [before] my own family ... I stood. And the path
> of the wise I seized and these things that the Twin had taught
> me, I then began to tell and to teach (my) father and the elders
> of the family. And when they heard (this), they were astonished.
> And just as a wise man who may find and plough the seed of
> a good and fruitful tree in untilled soil ... and bring it to [well-]
> tilled and cared for soil...."

> [M 49 II, Middle Persian: *MM* II, pp. 307-308; *Cat.* p. 5 (cf. M 464 a
> and M 3414)]

R I   You have come in peace,
        (you) vivifier of the souls,
        Lord Mani, Apostle of
        Light. You have come in
        peace, deliverer of
        the souls. You have come in
        peace, great redeemer,
        you have come in peace, shepherd...

R II   You have come in peace, brilliant collector (?),
        You have come
        in peace, powerful and
        strong. You have come in peace,
        best friend of the Lights.
        You have come in peace, sovereign
        of the religion. You have come in
        peace, beautiful (?) body.
        You have come in peace, ... name (?)

V I   peace, dearest and
        most beloved. Peace (be) upon
        your twin and your glory that
        went out with you. You have come
        in peace, co-twin
        of the gods, peace upon
        the Light gods, from whom
        you were born. You have come in (peace).

V II   You have (come) in peace, messenger of
        joy. Peace upon
        those understanding the message
        they hear from you. You have come in
        peace, beautiful and
        dearest name. Peace upon
        the fortunate that
        pay homage in front of you. (You) have come...

[Pelliot M. 914.2, Middle Persian: Jean de Menasce, "Fragments mani-
chéens de Paris," *W.B. Henning Memorial Volume* (London, 1970), p. 304 f.]

The doctrine of redemption brought by Mani to men was
consciously syncretistic. He admitted this openly; indeed, he empha-

sized it. He had come to bring together the heritage of Buddha, Zarathustra, Jesus and all former prophets to distill the real, the only true cognition. He was "the seal of the prophets," *khātimu'n-nabīyīn*, the man who brought the final answer, because:

> The religion that I (i.e., Mani) have chosen is in ten things above and better than the other, previous religions. Firstly: the primeval religions were in one country and one language. But my religion is of that kind that it will be manifest in every country and in all languages, and it will be taught in far away countries.
>
> Secondly: the former religions (existed) as long as they had the pure leaders, but when the leaders had been led upwards (i.e., had died), then their religions fell into disorder and became negligent in commandments and works. And in... [But my religion, because of] the living [books(?)], of the Teachers, the Bishops, the Elect and the Hearers, and of wisdom and works will stay on until the End.
>
> Thirdly: those previous souls that in their own religion have not accomplished the works, will come to my religion (i.e., through metempsychosis), which certainly will be the door of redemption for them.
>
> Fourthly: this revelation of mine of the two principles and my living books, my wisdom and knowledge are above and better than those of the previous religions.
>
> Fifthly: all writings, all wisdom and all parables of the previous religions when they to this [religion of mine came...]

[T II D 126 = M 5794, Middle Persian: *MM* II, pp. 295-96; *Cat.* p. 115]

Mani did bring to perfection what Zarathustra, Buddha, Jesus, and all prophets before them imperfectly had tried to teach, even if Vahman, the protector and personification of the Manichaean Church had given them a particle of the true knowledge:

> ... and hereafter, time after time, the Holy Ghost (i.e., Vahman) also proclaimed his greatness through the mouth of the primeval prophets, who are: Shem, Sem, Enosh, Nikotheos ... and Enoch. Until... and he was [a sower] of the seed of [Truth]. Just as you...

[M 299 a, Middle Persian: W. Henning, "Ein manichäisches Henochbuch," *SPAW* 1934, pp. 27-28; *Cat.* p. 21; cf. H.S. Nyberg, *W.B. Henning Memorial Volume* (London, 1970), p. 344]

The Holy Ghost also took as his mounts: Simon (i.e., Peter)

... James, Cephas (i.e., Simon Peter again), Mariam, Martha, Paul, Peter (i.e., Simon Peter for the third time), Thecla, BHYR (?) ... and Hermas the shepherd (instead of "The shepherd (pastor) of Hermas"). And they became apostles in the various lands and kept the religion (dyn) in a state of purity.

[M 788, R 2-8, Middle Persian: W.B. Henning, "The Murder of the Magi," *JRAS*, 1944, p. 142, n. 1; *Cat.* p. 53]

Direct polemics against other religions, therefore, were on the whole unnecessary. When polemical passages do occur in Manichaean literature, the intention in most cases is to stress a general disgust of idolatry and dogmatic abnormities:

... we will go out of [the land of] the sinners to the land of the beneficent. The young disciple says: "Well-being to all people who want and ask for this." [Well-be]ing also to you who wish [that] you could make [your] mind patient and understand what is revealed [to] you: the deceit of the dogmas — the teaching of the Gods (?), life — and death, piety and its teacher — sinfulness and its sower. Listen, delicate mankind! Direct eye and face (towards this and see) how it is depicted here (?) in front of you! On this picture: idols, idol priests, altars and their god. Close (lit., collect) my mind (to impressions from them): the sacrament(s), the profession, and the belief in them.

I will send the preaching ... they raise their voice like dogs. Truth is not in their speech. But you, know your own Self! Seize the road of the Gods! Now in the first place, [at] the head of all these (things) that are depicted here (?), this is the temple of the idols, which they call "The Dwelling of the Gods." And corresponding to the name of the dwelling, there are many (?) "gods" (there)! Many are running about, (and) when you ask: "Where (are you going)?" they say: "To 'The Dwelling of the Gods'! To offer reverence, love, gifts in front of them!" The idol priests raise their voice: "Come forth to 'The Dwelling of the Gods'!" However, inside "The Dwelling of the Gods" there are no gods! The deceived do not realize that, because their spirits have been made intoxicated. But you...

[M 219, Middle Persian: *MM* II, pp. 311-12 (cf. *BBB* p. 79, *BSOAS* XI, 1946, p. 725, and *BSOAS* XIV, 1952, p. 518); *Cat.* p. 16]

Another polemical text, however, has a clear target: and do not also those that worship the blazing fire know by this very fact that their end belongs to fire? And they assert that Ohrmizd

and Ahrmēn are brothers. It is consistent with such ideas that
they will come to an evil end.

Falsehood and slander they tell against Ohrmizd:
that Mahmi,[28] the demon, had taught him to make the
world light.

They murder and cut to pieces the creatures of Ohrmizd and
Ahrmēn:
they have been hostile to both the Families.

[M 28 I, R I, 33-R II, 13, Middle Persian: W.B. Henning, *Zoroaster,
Politician or Witch-Doctor?* (London, 1951), p. 50, n. 1; *Cat.* p. 4]

Zurvanism, a special form of Sasanian Zoroastrianism, by
emphasizing Zurvan, Time, as the first principle, father of *both*
Ohrmizd and Ahrmēn / Ahriman, had put the good god into
an unworthy position. This could only be considered lie and
deceit, the set name of any idolatry, as will appear from the same
text:

The countries are bewildered by deceptive idols, wall-pictures
made of wood and stone! They fear Deceit, they prostrate
themselves and pay homage to him. They have left the Father
in Heaven and worship Deceit.

[M 28 I, R I, 5-13:(*MM* II, p. 311, note 2); *Cat.* p. 4 (cf. H.W. Bailey,
Zoroastrian Problems in the Ninth-Century Books, Oxford 1943, p. 214)]

Also the Christians were guilty of blasphemy by calling
ṭhe son of Mary (bar Maryam) the Son of the Lord (*pus i
Adōnay*), for

If He (Adonay) is the Lord of everything, who did crucify His
Son?

But

To shame will at last be put all who worship idols.

[M 28 I, R II, 24 ff.; V I, 32-34: *HR* II, pp. 94-95; *Cat.* p. 4]

For

Because of empty tastes and livelihoods of the stomach, their
hand struck (their) Self with great destruction.

[M 28 I, V II, 28-32; *MM* II, p. 314, note 8; *Cat.* p. 4]

And striking one's Self is the same as striking the Divine!

The extent of that kind of text was indeed very moderate as
compared with the amount of writings *against* Manichaeism, for
centuries considered by the Christians the heresy *par excellence*.

When this literature is honest, as for instance in the case of Augustine of Hippo, it constitutes a very important source material, indicating not only what was found unjustifiable in Mani's teaching by his opponents, but also fundamental elements of this teaching. A good evidence in this respect is in one of Augustine's Letters (*Epistola* 236, 2):

> The Hearers eat meat and cultivate lands, and, if they wish, have wives, none of which things is allowed to the Elect. The Hearers go on their knees before the Elect, humbly begging the imposition of their hands. They join them in adoring and praying to the sun and the moon. They fast with them on Sundays, and along with them they believe all the blasphemous tenets which make the Manichaean heresy so detestable. Thus they deny Christ's birth of a virgin, and say that his flesh was not true flesh, but false, that his passion accordingly was mere pretence, and his resurrection null. They speak evil of the patriarchs and the prophets. They say that the law, given by God's servant Moses, was not given by the true God, but by the Prince of Darkness. They consider all souls (i.e., here the Living Self, *viva anima*), not only of men, but even of beasts, to be of the substance of God, and altogether parts of God. Finally, they say that the good and true God (i.e., the Father of Greatness through the First Man, Ohrmizd) entered into conflict with the race of Darkness, and mingled a part of himself with the Princes of Darkness, which part is defiled all the world over, but is purified by the meals of the Elect and by the sun and moon; while any portion of deity which it has been found impossible thus to purify is bound with an everlasting bond of punishment at the end of the world. Thus God is believed to be not only liable to violation and contamination and corruption, seeing that a portion of him is reducible to such misery, but to be unable even at the end of the world to get himself wholly cleansed from that so great defilement and uncleanness and misery.

Such words could not affect the pious Manichaean. To him they were classed with the religious distortions and perversions of idolatry, things that were the more terrifying as the true religion that gave salvation, had come and appeared, with its joyful message, in the holy books of Mani. *He*, contrary to other prophets, to Zarathustra, Buddha, Jesus, had committed his doctrine to a series of treatises, all save one (the Middle Persian *Shāhbuhragān*, "The

Shāhpuhr Book," one of the first, dedicated to the Sasanian Shāh-puhr I and mainly of eschatological content) written in his Eastern Aramaic mother tongue.

The canon itself was divided into seven parts, but it is uncertain whether or not *Shāhbuhragān* was included. With this book the other six parts are   1) *The Living* (or *Great*) Gospel,   2) *The Treasure of Life;*   3) *Pragmateia* (i.e., "Tract, Treatise");   4) *The Book of Secrets;*   5) *The Book of the Giants,* in which the story of the fallen angels (see 1 *Moses* 6) from the *Book of Enoch* played a great part; and   6) *Letters.* As however the canon catalogues among the Chinese and Coptic Manichees leave out the *Shāhpuhr Book,* this very probably stood alone. In that case, the seventh canonical section must have included *psalms* and *prayers.* The non-canonical literature includes the traditional Coptic *Kephalaia, homilies* and *collections of hymns,* as well as *Ārdahang,* a picture book illustrating the more important aspects of the doctrine. This immense confidence in the written tradition was something quite exceptional in the history of antiquity that never questioned the reliability and security of the oral tradition. Already in Plato (*Phaedrus*) we read the story of the Egyptian god Theuth, whose invention of letters was severely disapproved by Thamus, the King. And, to take just one more example, the great Zoroastrian work, the *Dēnkart,* without hesitation states that the living spoken word is much more important than the written one.

II. The Missionary Work

Manichaeism was not only definitive but universal and — with the authority of truism — proselytizing. The command of mission came from Mani himself, who travelled widely to propagate his gospel. His travels cannot be mapped in detail but he went to India, to what is nowadays Baluchistan, and to several other parts of ancient Iran. The Manichaean fragments relating the missionary history, of which there are quite a few, place great emphasis on the conversions of rulers which were achieved. Special glamour was attached to the benevolence with which Pērōz, the younger brother of Shāhpuhr I, who had taken over the previous office of the King of Kings as governor of Khorasan, met the new religion. It was undoubtedly Pērōz who arranged the first meeting between Mani and Shāhpuhr. On this occasion a friendly relationship developed between the two men which, judging by all sources, remained stable throughout the whole reign of Shāhpuhr. Mani was received "with great honors" and later made his appearance as a royal attendant over a prolonged period (according to the Coptic *Kephalaia* 15). This seems to be a reference to one of the campaigns against the Roman Empire, most likely under Valerian whose name was mentioned by the anti-Manichaean Alexander of Lycopolis (about the year 300) in connection with a comment that Mani "fought together with the Persian Sapor (Shāhpuhr)."

The reign of Shāhpuhr's son Hormizd I was too short (about one year) for Mani to find out exactly what the situation was, but in any case the position of the new religion was tolerable. This religion, called *"Righteousness"* (e.g., the Coptic *Homilies* 67, 22, and the Parthian M 4575) was quickly introduced into the whole area of the eastern and central Mediterranian, into Syria, Palestine (e.g., the mission of the Manichaean Julia in Ghaza, described by Marcus Diaconus in his *Life of Porphyrios*), and into Northern Arabia. In Egypt the communities were at an early date so predominant that the Sasanian Narsēs, otherwise despised by the Manichaeans, apparently tried to use them politically against the Romans, although it is uncertain under what circumstances. The religion was spread further into North Africa (St. Augustine), Armenia, Asia Minor, Dalmatia (the tomb inscription of the Lydian Bassa who was *parthenos*, "Virgin," i.e., one of the Elect) and into Rome (the *Liber Pontificalis* of Pope Miltiades, early fourth century).

The fourth century became the great Manichaean century in the West, judging by the almost feverish anti-Manichaean activities which found expression in a large number of polemic writings, in particular by Augustine towards the end of the century, and to some extent in edicts — continuing the edict of Diocletian of 297 — on the part of the ruling emperors Constantine the Great (326), Valentinian (372), and Theodosius (381-383). A considerable part of this success was due to the corps of missionaries working with the intuition of a genius and whom Mani himself had started off on their missions. Among the great names in the west are Mar Sisin who became Mani's sucessor after a five year interregnum and who therefore had obviously not been apointed by the Apostle himself; further Addai, Patēg (Pattikios), Innaios (Sisin's successor), Mar Zakō, Mar Gabriab and Abzakhya. But by the sixth century the decline had set in which gradually reduced western Manichaeism to a minimum. The center was shifted to the eastern regions of the Sasanian Empire Abar-shahr, Marw and the Balkh district. With the introduction of Parthian as the official language of the Religion, Mar Ammō, who had been sent out by Mani, established here a solid foundation for further expansions towards the East. Legend has it that the Central Asian Manichaeism, called *Dēnā-variyya*, was founded as an institution by Ammō. Historically, however, it goes back to Mar Shad Ohrmizd who died around the year 600. As Sogdian was the main language and Sogdian merchants became advocates of this religion, it penetrated further and further east and reached its culmination in prestige and importance when, for the first and only time in the history of Manichaeism, it was made the state religion by an official act of Bögü Khaghan in 762-763 under the Turkish Uighurs.

Texts from the Manichaean Missionary-History

And when the Tūrān-Shāh (i.e., the Prince of Turan in north eastern Baluchistan) saw that the Beneficent one (i.e., Mani) had got up, then he, indeed, from afar was on his knees. And

he implores the Beneficent one and speaks to him respectfully:
"Do not come hither before me!" Then the Beneficent one
went there. He (the prince) stood up and went to meet him.
And he kissed him. Then he says to the Beneficent one: "You
are the Buddha, and we are sinful men; it is not becoming
that you come to us. Because of that ... . As many steps as
w[e come] before you, [so much merit and] salvation will be
to us. And as many steps as you come to us, so much non-merit
and sin will be to us." Then the Beneficent one gave him his
blessing. And he says to him: "Be blessed! Just as you now on
earth amongst men are full of glory and honored, in that
very same way you on the last day of the soul, in the eyes of
the gods, shall be full of glory and noble. And among the gods
and the beneficent [Righ]teous (viz. in, paradise) you shall
be immortal for ev[er and ever]." Then ... he seized the hand ...

[M 8286, Parthian: W. Sundermann, "Zur frühen missionarischen Wirksamkeit Manis," *AOH* 24 (1971): p. 103-104; *Cat.* p. 135]

... the Apostle led the Righteous one (i.e., here, in a vision,
most probably one of the saved from paradise) up into the atmosphere (and)said: "What is (still) higher?" The Righteous one
said: My sphere!" The apostle said: "Fur[ther, what] is (still)
greater?" He said: "The earth that bears everything." Further
he said: "What is (still greater than these (things)? "The
Righteous one said: "The sky...". ... "What is (still) greater?"
He said: "The s[un] and the moon." "Further, what is (still)
lighter?" He said: "The wisdom of the B[uddha]." Then the
Tūrān-Shāh said: "Of all these you are the greatest and lightest,
for, in truth, you are the Buddha yourself." Then the Devout
one [said] to the Tūrān-Shāh: "You shall act so ..." ... apostles
have come to various countries, pious and sinner, and the actions
of the Electus and the [Hearer]. Then, when the Tūrān-[Shāh
and] the noblemen heard this word. they became happy,
adopted the belief and became well-disposed towards the
Apostle and the religion. Further, when the Tūrān-Shāh was
[with Mani in the gar]den (?), he found the [dau]ghter of the
Tūrān-Shāh and the brothers transported. Then the brothers
said their prayers to the Devout one, and the Apostle told the
Tūrān-Shāh a parable: "There was a man, and there were
seven sons. When the time of death had come, he called his
sons. Seven primeval ... and ..."

[M 48 I, M 1306 II, M 5911, M 1307, Parthian: W. Sundermann, "Weiteres,
zur frühen missionarischen Wirksamkeit Manis," *AOH* 24 (1971): 372-73;
Cat. pp. 5, 69, and 171]

... when our father (i.e., Mani) came from India (Hindūgān)
and arrived at the town of Rēv-Ardashīr (in the province of
Fārs (Pārs, Persis), near the Persian Gulf), then he sent the
Presbyter Patēg together with the brother Hannī to India,
to Dēb (till far into the Middle Ages the most important port
of the Indus delta). And he himself said at that time: "This
religion (lit., righteousness, *ardāwīft*) of mine is so blessed
[that] in every country — "
On ... From those having come (to him) he collected (his)
share. But it was not, what he had thought. When then the
Beneficent one a second time was in the town of Rēv-Ardashīr,
then a great man from Abar-shahr (i.e., the upper countries,
the eastern districts of the Sasanian Empire, in distinction to the
lower countries, Iraq), by the name of Dāryāv, came up before
him, he himself together with two other brothers Valāsh and
Khusrō. What he ... And when he ... he would not take (his)
share, and he did not say anything to me ... I went off and
in[creased] (his) share on[ce more] ..."

[From M 4575, Parthian: W. Sundermann,"Zur frühen missionarischen
Wirksamkeit Manis," *AOH* 24 (1971): 82-87; brought to light too late
to be listed in *Cat.*]

The Mēshūn-Shāh Mihrshāh

Moreover Shāhpuhr, the King of Kings, had a brother, Lord
of Mēshūn (i.e., Mesene, a district of Basra in Mesopotamia),
and his name was Mihrshāh. And to the religion of the Apostle
he was extraordinarily hostile. And he had arranged a garden,
which was good, lovely and extraordinarily large, so that there
was none like it. Then the Apostle knew that the time of salvation had come near. He then rose and appeared before Mihrshāh
who with great merriment was seated at a feast in the garden.
Then the Apostle ... he commanded. Then he said [to] the
Apostle: "Was there (ever) in the paradise that you praise,
such a garden as this garden of mine?" Then the Apostle understood this utterance of disbelief. Then by (his) miraculous
power he showed (him) the Paradise of Light with all gods,
divine beings and the immortal breath of life and every kind
of garden and also other splendid things there. Thereafter
he fell to the ground unconscious for three hours, and what he
saw he kept as a memory in his heart. Then the Apostle put
his hand upon his head. He regained consciousness. When he
had risen, he fell down at the Apostle's feet (and) seized his
right hand. And the Apostle said this ...

[M 47 I, Parthian: *HR* II, p. 82-84 (cf. *BBB* p. 103); *Cat.* p. 5]

And when the Apostle (Mani) was [in] Vēh-Ardashīr (i.e., Seleucia, on the western bank of the Tigris), then [he sent] ... the Teacher, Adda the Bishop ... [and] other scribes to Byzans, [and he gave them] four instructions ... and writings of Light ... refutations of dogmas he made and arranged in many w[ays], after ... the religions. And all he ... and put to shame. [Like] one who the weapon of the powerful...

[M 216 c, Parthian: *MM* II, p. 301, n. 2, and p. 302, n. 3 (cf. *BBB* p. 111); *Cat.* p. 16]

... [he saw] the figure of the Apostle and fell on his face and became unconscious. The people were [amazed]. Thereupon they prayed: "To us ... Jesus ... we shall ...." ... he overcame the teachings of the (other) religions by their own evil. Havazā (?), the Varuchān-Shāh (Varuchān probably a district near Balkh) [said]: "What is all this talk about?" And they said: "It is ... but ...." Havazā...

[M 216 b, Parthian: W.B. Henning, "Waručān = Sâh," *Journal of the Greater India Society* 11 (1944): 85-86; *Cat.* p. 16]

The Coming of the Apostle into the Countries

"... become familiar with the writings!" They went to the Roman Empire (and) saw many doctrinal disputes with the religions. Many Elect and Hearers were chosen. (The Presbyter) Patēg was there for one year. (Then) he returned (and appeared) before the Apostle. Hereafter the Lord sent three scribes, the *Gospel* and two other writings to Adda (Addai), He gave the order: "Do not take it farther, but stay there like a merchant who collects a treasure." Adda laboured very hard in these areas, founded many monasteries, chose many Elect and Hearers, composed writings and made wisdom his weapon. He opposed the "dogmas" with these (writings), (and) in everything he acquitted himself well. He subdued and enchained the "dogmas." He came as far as Alexandria. He chose Nafshā [29] for the Religion. Many wonders and miracles were wrought in those lands. The Religion of the Apostle was advanced in the Roman Empire. Then, when the Apostle of Light was in the city of Holvān,[30] he called Mar Ammō, the Teacher, who knew the Parthian script and language (and) also was familiar with .... He sent him to Abarshahr together with Prince Ardavān and brethren who were scribes, (and) a miniature painter. He said: "Blessed be this Religion, may it be advanced in greatness there through Teachers, Hearers, and Soul Service.[31] And may for you ... name be ... of heart; may the great Vahman keep (you in) fortune and prosperity (more than) the previous (religions)."

And [32] they had arrived at the watch-post of Kushān, then the
spirit of the border of the Eastern Province appeared in the
shape of a girl, and he (i.e., the spirit) asked me: "Ammō,
what do you intend? From where have you come?" I said:
"I am a believer, a disciple of Mani, the Apostle." That spirit
said: "I do not receive you. Return (to the place) from where
you have come." And he disappeared from me. Then I, Ammō,
stood, fasting for two days, in praise in front of the Sun. Then
the Apostle appeared (and) said: "Do not be disheartened!
Read aloud in front (of the spirit) the (chapter) "The Assembling of the Gates" [34] from (the book) *The Treasure of the Living!*
Then, the next day that spirit appeared (again), said to me:
"Why have you not returned to your own country?" I said:
"From a place far away I have come for the sake of the Religion." That spirit said: "What is the Religion that you bring?"
I said: "We do not eat flesh nor drink wine, from [women] we
keep far away." He said: "Where I rule ... there are many
like you!" Then I read aloud in front of (him) "The Assembling
of the Gates" of *The Treasure of the Living.* Then he did reverence
(to me and) said: "You are the pure righteous man. From now
on do not call yourself "man of religion," but "true bringer
of religion," you who have no equal." Then I asked: "What is
your name?" He said: "I am called Bag Ard, (and I am) the
frontier guard of the Eastern Province. When I receive you,
then the gate of the whole East will be opened in front of you".
Then the spirit Bag Ard taught me "The Assembling of the
Five Gates" by means of parables

"The gate of the eyes that is deceived when seeing what is
vain, (is) like unto the man who sees a mirage in the desert:
a town, a tree, water (and) many other things that demon
makes him imagine and kills him. Further (it is) like unto
a castle on a rock (?) to which the enemies found no access.
Then the enemies arranged a feast, much singing and music.
Those in the castle became greedy of seeing, (and) the enemies
assaulted them from behind and took the castle. The gate of
the ears (is) like unto that man who went along a secure (?)
road with many treasures. Then two robbers stood near his
ear, deceived him through beautiful words, took him to a place
far away and killed him (and) stole his treasures. Further
(it is) like unto a beautiful girl who was kept locked up in a
castle, and a deceitful man who sang a sweet melody at the
base of the castle wall, until that girl died of grief. The gate
of the smelling nose (is) like unto the elephant when it from
a mountain above the garden of the king became greedy of the

smell of the flowers, fell down from the mountains in the night and died. The gate of the (mouth is) like ..."

[M 2, Middle Persian: *MM* II, pp. 301-06; *Cat.* p. 1]

A Letter from a Manichaean church dignitary (Mar Sisin?) to — most probably — Mar Ammō

"you shall make no respite. On the contrary, you shall not delay what good you are able to do now, for time is running quickly. And you shall know thus: even if you had been here in Marw yourself — (yes), I cannot believe that your love and nobleness could have been so manifest in Marw as (is) now (the case) (i.e., in spite of you being absent). And you shall know thus: when I came up to Marw, then I found all brothers and sisters pious. And to the dear brother Zurvandad I am very, very grateful; because he with such piety has taken care of all brothers. And I have now let him go to Zamb[34] and sent him to dear Mar Ammō and Khorasan, and (the *Book of*) *the Giants* and the *Ardahang* he has taken with him. And I have made another (copy of the *Book of*) *the Giants* and the *Ardahang* in Marw. Further you shall know thus: when I came, I found Rashtin the brother so as I wanted. And as for piety and zeal he was (exactly) so as Mar Mani wants.

"... And ... I have written to you, because I know that you are glad of my kindness, and in order that they glorify God and Mar Mani: as long as I and you live, I will appoint Bishops and Teachers as watchmen in every city and province of the Upper Countries that also your name will be (honored) and this religion of Mar Mani everywhere may find leaders and advocates. [And], behold, the [dear] brother Khusrō I have sent to you.

... that you may be very glad. And you shall act so that you, as much as you can, labour for the Hearers, in order that, when I send brothers (to you), they will find (proper) reception. And as for Friyadar you shall know thus: he has been with me from the time he arrived, and he had [lo]ve and faith. And now he comes over to you. You, too, shall do thus: Receive him in joy and take care of him as if he were your own son, so that I also can be grateful to you. And, behold, I have let the beloved son of Mar Mani go to you. He comes to you in love so you too should receive him as you would your own son and teach him well in the art of the scribe and in wisdom. And you shall not withhold anything from these brothers that come to you. And if they desire (?) anything in wisdom, teach them so as if the they were your own children. And do not mind, (even) if they ask inconsiderate questions, but you shall know thus: There has never been any disciple that (at once) leaves school as a learned man. On the contrary, he learns day after day. There is (a disciple) who has a feeling and loves his teacher; and he follows him and loves his name and always acts nobly towards (his) teacher; and there is another disciple who (does) not (act) like that, but is hostile and becomes... (But) all one must tolerate in the same way. You, however, shall not turn away from anybody, but to all who offer you their hands, (you shall) in faith ..."

[T II D II 134 II = M 5815 II, Parthian: *MM* III, pp. 857-60; *Cat.* p. 115]

The motives of conversions of the kind described above to a religion, whose tendency to renounce life and state is obvious, are difficult to explain; but strong political ones cannot be ruled out. Perhaps in a religious-historic context the Manichaeism of Bögü Khaghan for instance should rather be considered as a somewhat insignificant intermezzo. With the development of semi-nomadism into urban culture (the Uighur kingdom of Khotsho, 850-1250), Buddhism alone seemed to be of decisive influence. In Tibet, towards the south, too, there is literary evidence of Manichaeism; but nothing further is known regarding its position and expansion. Owing to a correct written tradition, which also includes the imperial edicts, the situation in China is much clearer. In 694 and also in 719, a Manichaean priest of high standing was introduced at the imperial court; and already, 13 years after the last visit (732), it was considered necessary to reject Manichaeism ("Mo-mo-ni's (Mar Mani) Teachings") categorically. The freedom of the cult was permitted among such foreign peoples in the empire for whom this was their native religion. Later tolerance edicts (768 and 771) were, however, followed by strict prohibitions resulting immediately in bloody persecutions. Traces of Manichaeism (especially in the province of Fu-kien in Southern China) continued for several centuries but they seem to reveal a considerable degeneration and in some cases strongly Taoistic elements. The centre of the expansion was shifted somewhat towards the west with the coming of Islam, because Islam, being in favor of religions of the book, raised hopes for better times to come among many Manichaeans in the Persian empire as well as in Transoxiana.

This hope, however, was soon frustrated and the Manichaean renaissance in the west, which had been opened up, came to nothing. There is no doubt that all this was not entirely without importance for Muhammad's religion, but details of this development are not available. How obscure the image of the historical Mani became is evident from the fact that Mani, in the later Islamic tradition, was not remembered as founder of a religion or as the great religious personality, but pre-eminently as an artist. The image of Mani drawn by this tradition is completely dominated by the idea of the painter Mani, an essential feature of Manichaeism in general as well as of the person Mani thus being preserved for posterity. The tradition is historically well founded, partly in the Manichaeans' well-known care of and interest in paper, writing, and illustrations, partly in the existence of Mani's *Árdahang*, probably an appendix to, but different from, the *Living Gospel*.

According to this tradition Mani is a man from China, as already in Firdausi's *Shāh Nāmah* (about A.D. 1000) and in Gurgani's *Vis and Ramin* (eleventh century). It is the Central Asian tradition in its late western version, which is a result of the short, but to the elaboration of the Islamic concept of heresy very effective, renaissance of Manichaeism during the first centuries after Muhammad. But in its Persian form, this version degenerates into ravings or — in most cases — is secularized completely. The word "Mani" becomes an appellative which denotes a painter of great renown and with exceptional powers; and Mani himself appears as "the master," "the leader" of "the Chinese school of painters," the painter who bears comparison with the great Bihzād from Herat. As late as the beginning of the present century, when Sanᶜatizāde Kirmānī wrote his "Narrative about Mani the Painter" which, with his other writings and especially Jamālzāde's *Yakī būd - yakī nabūd*, and the purely social novels from the beginning of the 1920s, characterized and introduced the new dawn in Persian literature, it is the tradition about the artist which alone determined Mani's posthumous literary reputation.

III. Hearers and Elect:
the Manichaean Community

One condition for the fast Manichaean expansion leading to its culmination in the eighth century was its firm hierarchic structure centering around Mani's successors and their residence, which was in Babylon up to the tenth century and after that in Samarkand. The primacy of Mani's successors was uncontested, although the Manichaean religion did not escape schismatic troubles altogether. One case, reported by Ibn an-Nadim, and placed by him in the eighth century, is confirmed by Manichaean Sogdian letter fragments from Turfan. Below the actual dignatories was the community, divided into five classes:

1) 12 apostles or teachers

2) 72 bishops

3) 360 priests (*mahistag, presbyter*)

4) the Elect (male and female)

5) Hearers (male and female)

All Manichaeans holding offices (apostles, bishops, priests) were, of course, Electi, "upper-class," corresponding with for instance the Buddhist monks who with the aid of the laity were enabled to live the religiously perfect life. The number of apostles and bishops undoubtedly followed the Christian practice. Christian writers from the fourth century and ownards were aware of this similarity and openly state that when Mani chose the number twelve he followed the example of the Church. The same can probably also be said of the number of the bishops because there was evidence of the same changing numbers between 70 and 72 among the Manichaeans as are testified for Christianity in the manuscript-text groups for *Luke* 10, 17.

TEXTS CONCERNING THE HEARERS, THE ELECT, AND THE HIERARCHY

Precepts for Hearers

... they kill ... even on those who ... them, they shall have mercy so that they do not kill them in the same way as the wicked kill (them). But dead flesh of any animals, wherever they find it, be it (naturally) dead or slaughtered, they may eat; and whenever they find it, either through trading or as a livelihood or as a present, they may eat (it). And that is enough for them. This is the first precept for Hearers. And the second precept (is) that they shall not be false, and that they, one towards the other, (shall) not (be) unjust ... and they shall walk (?) in truth. And the Hearer shall love the Hearer in the same way as one loves one's own brother and relatives, for they are children of the Living Family (i.e., the whole Manichaean community) and the World of Light. And the third precept is that they shall not slander anybody and not be false witness(es) against anybody of what they have not seen, and not make an oath in falsehood in any matter and lie and...

[T II D 126 II = M 5794 II, Middle Persian: *MM* II, pp. 296-97; *Cat.* p. 115]

Exhortations for Hearers

... thus it is fitting that he (i.e., a man of the world wanting to become a Hearer), just as he gives himself up to hate and protects (defends) the country (viz. as a soldier) and does agriculture and makes payment(s) and eats flesh and drinks wine and has wife and child and acquires house and property and assembles for the body (i.e., takes care of worldly things instead of concentrating on the salvation of the soul) and pays tax in the country and robs and damages and proceeds with oppression and mercilessness — (it is fitting that he) in the same way should also ask for the wisdom and knowledge of the gods and think of the soul. And also the one (who) more truly ... the affairs... and does and ... house and ... tru(ly) ... (the persons over) whom he (the Hearer) has (authority), he shall keep away from lewdness and fornication and evil thinking, evil speaking and evil doing; and he (himself) shall also keep his hand away from robbery and damage and violence and mercilessness and always keep away from soil and water and fire and trees and plants and wild and tame animals (viz. because of the particles of Light in them) and hurt them (as) little (as possible). For they, too, live on (towards salvation) by the help of that Light

and Goodness of God (viz. that was mixed with Darkness).
Like that warrior and worker and ... also and soul ... is ... and ...

[M 49 I, Middle Persian: *MM* II, pp. 306-307; *Cat.* p. 5]

On the Hearers and the Elect

...by the help of the Soul Service and by the help of ... [and]
friendship they become bound up with them (i.e., the Elect)
and with all their heart they strive for friendship (with them)
and they love them so as if they were their relatives.

And through these two signs they are connected with them:
through the sign of love and through the sign of fear, (the
signs) that they receive from them, and they show them their
respect in such a way as one may do towards one's master and
lord, and they fear to ignore their command and (not) to believe
in these hidden things (i.e., the teaching that is opened, explained to them by the Elect)and Greatnesses (i.e., the gods)
that they at all times hear of from them. And in the same way
they also fear and avoid evil conduct and greediness. [And]
as for knowledge they certainly(?) are greatly bound up (with
them).

In the commandments and acts, however, they are s[till] inferior; because they [are] bound up with the action of the world
and with the covetousness of lust and with the desire of men
and women [and] (because they) through pregnancy and birth
of ... (and through) ... of go[ld and s]ilver and ... And, therefore, [because the Hearers] are inferior to the Righteous (the
Elect), for that reason there will for them be no stop in the
transmigration (of souls) before they, when and where it is
fitting for them, are disengaged from evil doing, on account
of this that they have not abandoned world and sin in the same
perfect way as the Righteous have done. For the Righteous
have abandoned the whole world and its covetousness and have
become perfect through that one and only hankering after
being made divine.

[And through these] two signs they (i.e., the Hearers together
with the Elect) in truth stand in one mind, through the sign
of love and through the sign of fear, for this reason: because
they have abandoned all covetousness and all transmigration
and agony [and a]ll distress and annihilation and are redeemed
without defilement and go off and [are] received and collected
in that great and praised Realm [and] in that Light of....

[T III D 278 II = M 8251 I, Middle Persian: *MM* II, pp. 308-11; *Cat.*
p. 135]

"That one is a Righteous *Dēndār* (Electus) who saves many people from hell, and sets them on the way to paradise. And now I command you, Hearers, that so long as there is strength in your bodies, you should strive for the salvation of your souls. Bear in mind my orders and [my words], that straight path and true mould which I have shown to you, viz. the sacred religion. Strive through that mould so that you will join me in the eternal life."

Thereupon all the Hearers became very joyful and happy on account of the divine words and priceless orders which they had heard from the Apostle, the Lord Mar Mani. They paid exquisite homage, and received the...

[M 135 B, Sogdian: W.B. Henning, "Sogdian Tales," *BSOAS* 11 (1945); 469 f.; *Cat.* p. 11]

And some Hearers are like unto the juniper which is ever green, and whose leaves are shed neither in summer nor in winter. So also the pious Hearer, in times of persecution and of free exercise (lit. openmindedness), in good and bad days, either far from the Elect or near to them, — he is constant in his charity and faith.

[M 171 I V, 9-17, Parthian: W.B. Henning, "The Book of the Giants," *BSOAS* 11 (1943); 63, n. 6; *Cat.* p. 13]

The Hearer who gives alms (to the Elect), is like unto a poor man that presents his daughter to the king; he reaches (a position of) great honour. In the body of the Elect the (food given to him as) alms is purified in the same manner as a ... that by fire and wind ... beautiful clothes on a clean body ... turn....

[From M 101 f, Middle Persian: W.B. Henning, *BSOAS* 11 (1943); 59, 63 f.; *Cat.* p. 9]

On the Hierarchy and the Community

May they in every country and district where they come, protect the communities of the Elect and the monasteries ... pious... More and more (may blessing come) over you, Teacher [of the good name], you who are seated on the throne of the Prophets. You are the head and the leader, a good holder of the throne, a ... of the apostles, a sympathetic father and our loving [mother]. (You are) the one that directs us in love and sends us to that joy and life of the fortunate. You are the lord and fortunate sovereign, the bestower of all virtues to the children who hope for you. May now for you increase glory upon glory, health and victory, joy and virtue, growth and help, brilliance and beauty from this Ancestor, whose heritage is ours for ever and ever.

72 bishops of truth, the teachers of the road of peacefulness (i.e., the true religion, Mani's religion): may also for them glory and joy increase, and may their fame be furthered through praise in every flock and district.

360 house-masters (i.e., priests, presbyters), the very great nourishers of the children of the gods, the offspring of Lord Mani: may they be happy and joyful through ever new increase of devoutness and happiness.

The wise preachers, the teachers and revealers of the secrets of wisdom, the flute-players of Vahman [Narim]an through the sign of the First-Called One (i.e., the First Man) ..., the good scribes (i.e., from among the Elect), the sons of the gods, the strong men, the apostles of the spirit, the pure girls (i.e., the female Elect) who do and complete the will of their saviour, [may they achieve] invulnerability and obtain the fame of ...

All pure Elect, the shining (?) lambs, the pigeons of white feathers, mourn, lament and are grieved over the Highest Self (i.e., the Living Self), the Son of Jesus the Friend and they sing of the Living Spirit (i.e., the Holy Ghost). Blessed be — that the Sisters (i.e., the female Hearers) may be perfected with completeness — the Holy Girls, the brides of the Light Bridegroom (i.e., Jesus); may they be protected through the Right Hand of Health (i.e., Jesus) and go to the Land of the Living.

May the Hearers of the living word, those of the good soul, the fences of the holy religion, increase in all happiness and blessing and become perfect through the command of the saviour.

The monasteries and abodes of the Gods, the ... places and cabins, where Light Vahman fulfils the desire of becoming divine: the powerful Gods, the strong Apostles, the mighty Church leaders, the Glories, the Spirits (i.e., guardian angels), the Sons of the Right Hand who have entered them, may they come (?) in peace. Peace and blessing over these blessed gardens of fragrant flowers and ... .

Blessed be God, Light, Power and Wisdom (i.e., "the Four-faced Father of Greatness" as a Greek abjuration formula has it) that they themselves may increase ever new health and peace for the whole Holy Religion and for the fortune [and w]ell-being of all of us.

[M 36, Middle Persian: *MM* II, p. 323-316; *Cat.* p. 4. See A. Périkhanian, "Notes sur le lexique iranien et arménien," *RÉA*, n.s. 5, 1968, p. 16 ('z'dyy)]

Elegy on the Death of Mar Zakō

... Shepherd. O Great Lamp that swiftly died away: black turned our eye, languid and ...?. O Hero, Battle-stirrer who left (his) army: terror seized the troop, and the military column was confused. O Great Tree whose stature was broken: tremor came to the birds, whose nest was destroyed. O Great Sun who turned away from (this) world: dark became our eye, for the light was hidden.

O Greatest Caravan-leader who left (his) caravan in deserts, plains, mountains, and valleys. O Heart and Soul that vanished from us: we want your skill, reason, and glory! O Living Sea that became dry: the course of the rivers was held back ,and they do not run any longer. O Green Mountain where sheep graze: the milk for the lambs was finished, sorrowfully the sheep are sighing. O Mighty Father whose many sons are suffering, all the children that have become orphans. O Lord who spared no pains, who was in want; in everything he kept the house of God thriving. O Great Spring whose source has been closed: the sweet refreshment was held back from our mouth. O Bright Lamp whose light splendor shone towards others: to us came dusk(?). O Mar Zakō, Shepherd, Fortunate Teacher, without reason separation from you now (?) came to us. We shall not any longer look into you shining eyes and not any longer listen to your sweet words - O God Srōshāv [34] (i.e., the Father of Greatness, see p. 48), with the sweet name, Brilliant Lord, there is no one like You among all gods - We are depressed, sorrowfully we sigh, weep, we will always remember your (i.e., now again Mar Zakō) love. You were the throne-keeper in all realms, sovereigns and magnates reverenced you. Lovely and kind (was your) nature, mild your talk that never showed bitter anger.

Great Giant, strong in patience, you tolerated everybody, you were renowned. Righteous, innocent, merciful, giftful, generous, compassionate, kind father, who made happy the oppressed, (you) who saved numberless souls from distress (and) guided them to their home. Strong, good, powerful one, who, like all apostles, Buddhas and gods, found a throne. To you first I pay homage, I, the smallest of (your) sons who was left an orphan and an exile by you, Father.

Come hither, let us write a letter to the beneficent King of Light. From Him we will wish: Forgive our sins!

[M 6, Parthian: *MM* III, pp. 865-67; *Cat.* p. 2]

Parables and Stories on the Hearers

... wa[s] rich ... the noble
also all ... garment
as a gift, of much ornament, received.
They went, had a dinner, received gifts.
They became glad. (When) the sun went down, the man out of
contentment did not at once light the lamps.
The king became distrustful. Those near to him said:
"This man made a nice dinner, gave gifts; but
the lamps he did not light. If only he does not intend
committing a sin!" The man heard it, feared, became un-
[conscious.
Then the servants of this man
arranged a thousand lamps before the king. Then
the king was aware that the man was innocent. Out of
forgetfulness he had acted in that way, not in an
evil intention. The king blamed the man a little.
Then he gave (him) gifts (and) left (him) in friendship, goodness.
The interpretation: The poor man (viz. of rank/divine knowl-
[edge) is the Hearers.
The king (is) ... the royal messengers
went ... messenger (and) envoy
of the Gods [... ga]rden, vineyard, house,
shadow: it is the Soul Service. The Hearers render it to
the religion (and) build monasteries. Those near to
the king are the Elect. The garment
(and) ornament that he made are the (holy) picture(s) and
[book(s).
The lamp (is) the wisdom. The one that was not at once
lit is that of the Hearers.
Time after time they become slack in (their) action

and forgetful. There will be questioning.
Then they achieve victory, (and their) soul is saved.
The servants that lit the lamps (and)
helped the man, (that means:) the pious action
will help the Hearers. Just as the Hearers of this parable, if
they — be it possible — with (all their) heart
reverence the religion in love, become friends of the gods
(and) receive victory from the Glory of the religion (i.e.,
[Vahman)....

[M 47 II, Middle Persian: Ed. W. Sundermann, lines 1705-1739; *Cat.* p. 5]

A parable remarkable through the fact that it has been put into
a "historical" setting, is represented by this text, where Mani
himself appears as the teacher who shows the female Hearer Khybra
(the name is not clear) the sinfulness of mourning, because death
means release from the tyranny of matter:

On the Parable of the Hearer Khybra.
... were prepared. Then also that woman,
the mother of a girl, a bride, thinks:
"This woman who has a son, she
has prepared this for all, and I also have a
daughter. Now all that this woman
has made and prepared, is in the same way
becoming to do also for me." And also this woman began
just so to ar[range] ...
like this woman ...
just as she ...
six ...
me who until now did not know
that I, when I weep over the corporeal son,
kill the spiritual one.
But from now on I shall not weep and
(thus) I will not kill him." And she asked for forgiveness of
[her sin
and for love. Then
the Lord (Mani) blessed her greatly, and thereafter
... he went away [from] there and ...

[M 45, Middle Persian: Ed. W. Sundermann, lines 1740-1760; *Cat.* p. 5]

For a Hearer there was as a rule only one hope of salvation:
to deserve to be reborn as an Electus and then to go straight to
paradise. For in the everyday life of the Hearer the violation of
Light, in one way or another, could not be avoided, however
great generosity he showed towards the Elect, the generosity that
alone made it possible for those to be Elect. But there were some
exceptions, individual cases where the Hearer, by undertaking the
draconic decisions of the Elect and through a rigoristic self-
discipline, became the perfect Hearer, i.e., an Electus. He carries
the redeeming knowledge, the *Nous*, in himself. He comes to Vahman,
and Vahman comes to him — Vahman, the master of the congregation and the organizer of congregational life in as well as outside
the monastery. He was the one "who comes and appears to the
Holy Church", as the Coptic *Kephalaia* have it. The Elect, the
Hearers, and Vahman *are*, so to say, the Manichaean congregation.
It is Vahman who, with the Five Members (sense, reason, thought,
imagination, intention) and the Five Gifts (love, faith, perfecting,
patience, wisdom), creates the New Man receptive to acquirement
of gnosis. And it is Vahman, the personified Church, who guides
the soul upwards to paradise. This function, also among the
Zoroastrians, is attributed to Vahman (e.g., *Great Bundahishn*
163, 10); but in the Manichaean texts it is not exclusively reserved
for him.

> ... and like a highwayman
> [who] killed [tho]se sons, so are also
> all of you, who lay hands on the earth with
> ... and torture (it) in every way. And with your whole
> [body] you move over the earth and wound ... . And this
> Living [Self] from where you were born, you violate and
> injure. And over your hand it always weeps and complains.
> You Hearers who stand there with so much sin
> and offence, once for how many times are you in need (?) of
>   [absolution
> and mercy? Day after day from the Elect
> wish for meeting (?) and absolution
> [that] they ... bring mercy over you".

[M 580, Parthian: Ed. W. Sundermann, lines 2024-2035; *Cat.* p. 41]

But the Perfect Hearers:
They are like a man (who is) without pain
and healthy, who all over his body is without pain
and healthy, and nor is there other pain and suffering in
him. But at some limb
he scratches himself a little and gets up nervous [and]
turns constantly to it and considers when
it will be that this scratch will be healed so that
he will be healthy and painless all over the body"

[*Ibid.*, lines 2042-2049]

... to their own soul they become bene[ficent].
Firstly: they shall walk on together with the El[ect]
and hold their hand away from
destroying and injuring all
Light. Through this sole good action
they have become helpers of their own soul. And
secondly: they come to the sign and sight of
Light Vahman, who entered the Holy Church,
and pay homage to him and
render him praise and adoration. And
they know who he is, and to his greatness
and beauty they bear testimony. And
thirdly: through the sign of peace (i.e., Mani's Religion)
they walk amongst the peaceful and
keep far away from the border and boundary of the enemies
and are separated from those
false (?) ones that with the sign
of peace are not happy.

· · · · · · · · · · · · · · · · · ·

And through
the alms (given) by themselves, those Hearers
incorporate themselves into the Holy Church and
achieve the same share as the Elect. And a Hearer
that brings alms to the Elect
is like unto a poor man
to whom a pretty daughter has been born, and with charm
and nobleness she is very beautiful.

And that poor man
fosters the beauty of that girl, his
daughter, for she is very beautiful.
And that beautiful daughter he [adorns?]
and presents her to the king;
and the king approves of the girl; and he
himself takes her to wife. According to
the distri[bution of the Gods,] he has sons by her...
... The sons that he had by that
poor man's daughter... "

[From M 221, Middle Persian: Ed. W. Sundermann, lines 1977-1994 and,
cf. also W.B. Henning, *MM* II: 309, n. 1, and *BSOAS* 11 (1943): 64, n. 1,
2006-2023; *Cat.* p. 16]

IV. Manichaeism as Literary Intermediary

It was a matter of course that as representatives of the only perfect religion, Mani and the missionaries that came after him considered themselves fully entitled to take from other religions and cultures whatever they found useful to prepare the way for their own religion. With an aptitude for accommodation completely unknown in religious history before or since, they presented the doctrine in such a form that their listeners, whether Christian, Zarathustrian or Buddhist, could comprehend it immediately. In this zeal for their Religion, the Manichaeans obtained a not insignificant position as literary intermediaries. Considering the fact that Mani's religion fundamentally renounced life and regarded life on earth as a caricature and the body as a prison* for the soul that was now exiled, removed from the wonderful World of Light from which it originally came, and for which it longed with a never stilled longing, one might wonder at the joy of art of the Manichaeans, expressed in their masterly miniature paintings and Central Asian frescoes, their calligraphy, their ingeniously composed hymns and songs of an often refined symbolism, and their deep musical interest. But this joy and enthusiasm is first of all anticipating the heavenly delight and glory to come. If only this was kept in view, one might with a clear conscience take delight in the minstrel (gōsān)

> who proclaims the worthiness of kings and heroes of old

[Parthian; Mary Boyce, *JRAS*, 1957, p. 11]

even if his speech could never be as delicious as that of the great apostle, as that of e.g., the Prophet Enoch,

> who in (his) songs (is) [sweet]er than the minstrels *(hunivāzān)*

[From M 22, Middle Persian: W. B.Henning, *SPAW*, 1934, p. 28, n. 7; *Cat.* p. 3]

After all they sang of the joys of *this* world that was only a faint reflection of those of the coming world, of the Paradise of Light. Death, therefore, both as definitive and "temporary," is a good thing; and mourning and lamenting is a sin. The sinfulness of

mourning, an "Indo-European" motif, well-known from folk-
tales, was intensely realized by the Manichaeans. For the real
life, of course, was life in the Paradise of Light, the life and the world
one had in one's thought, even when apparently worldly songs
were used, and the life that the Living Self, a stranger in *our* world,
this world, so fervently wished for:

> The shining sun
> and the glittering full moon
> shine and glitter
> from the trunk of this tree.
> Brilliant birds
> are there sporting happily.
> Sporting (there) are doves (and)
> peacocks of all colours.

[M 554 b, Middle Persian: *HR* II, p. 69, Heinrich F. J. Junker, "Mittel-
pers. *frašēmurv*, 'Pfau'," *Wörter und Sachen* 12 (1929): 132; *Cat.* p. 39]

And the despair of the fettered Light Soul makes itself heard in
a Persian-Manichaean qaside in Islamic garment from the ninth
tenth century, "a witness to the adaptability of Manichaean
propaganda, to its readiness to assume ever fresh disguises in order
to meet the demands of the times," as Professor W.B. Henning
says in the preface to his ingenious reconstruction of the text:

> ... sated with water and juicy.
> Piteous [the creature] that is incapable of giving the Answer!
> [With the help of] the *Dhulfaqar* (i.e., the sword of Ali,
> presented to him by Muhammad, his father-in-law)
> of Reason do open your speech [in plaint]!
> I cry for help against this age, [against this tyranny of] mankind.
> I cry for help against this age, the age of quarrels and strife.
> ·   ·   ·   ·   ·   ·   ·   ·   ·   ·   ·   ·   ·   ·   ·   ·
> [Whenever] the wind of Virtue brings before me the
> wine of [Truth?], the simoom of [passion mingles
> with it illusion-creating] snake-poison.
> Ever [since] ... I was a horseman, I came to know
> for certain ... they bridle (?) four horses unsaddled.
> [They put] me, Noah-like, into an ark by force —

That (ark) which [is] ... more helplessly cast
down [on] shallows.
They throw me, Joseph-like, into the pit with violence —
that pit whence I shall only rise at the
time of (the last) reckoning.

[From M 786, Persian: W.B. Henning, "Persian Poetical Manuscripts from the Time of Rûdakî," *A Locust's Leg : Studies in Honour of S.H. Taqizadeh* (London, 1962), p. 100 ff.; *Cat.* p. 53]

The endeavour and attention of the religion, of Mani, and of the Elect to carry out the salvation of the dear soul is, perhaps, metaphorically expressed in this Old Turkish poem:

Like the grey wolf I will walk with you;
like the black raven I will stay on earth.
Like the charcoal to the disease,
like the spittle to the whetstone I will be.
You are our powerful great ruler.
Like gold rounded.
like a ball rounded,
you are our glorious wise lord.
And your numerous people
at your wide breast,
at your long seam
keeping and protecting, you nurse (and) take care of.

[P. Zieme, "Ein manichäisch-türkisches Gedicht," *Türk Dili Arastirmalari Yillği-Belleten,* 1968' den ayribasim (Ankara, 1969), p. 39 ff.]

The very fact of the Manichaeans' fully realizing the rich possibilities of use offered by foreign literatures in all regions where they wanted to propagate their teaching, made them outstanding literary intermediaries; their importance also to European intellectual life hardly can be over-estimated. Everything, so to say, could be used, even purely worldly matters; because the Manichaeans, as none previous to them, understood the art of adaptation and, in their fables and parables (āzind), were capable of taking advantage of it in the religious education: *Aesop* has supplied them with material. So has the Indian collection of tales the *Panchatantra,* the "Five Books," and, not least, those Buddha stories that, through the medium of Manichaeans (several texts in Uighur,

Parthian, and Persian (metrical) have been preserved), became one
of the "bestsellers" of *Christian* European literature, *Barlaam and
Joasaph* (Joasaph = Bodhisattva = (here) Buddha). This work was
attributed to St. John Damascene (eighth century) after having
been christianized, with an Arabic and a Georgian translation as
connecting links. Aesop was a happy choice! For according to the
rhetor Theon (second century A.D.) a fable was a "fictitious story
picturing a truth." With one exception, all Manichaean texts
deriving from the Aesop tradition are in Uighur (Old Turkish).
The Iranian exception, however, is not the least important one.
It is the famous fable about the jealous fox and the foolish
monkey, already known by the Greek poet Archilochos from
the seventh century B.C. and used again by the French La
Fontaine. Aesop has:

The Fox (alōpēx) and The Monkey (píthēkos)

Having danced and won favour before an assembly of animals,
a monkey was elected king by them. When the fox, being
jealous of him, saw a piece of meat in a snare, he took him there
and said that he had found a treasure; and, instead of using
it himself, he had kept it for him as a perquisite of his royal
office; and he invited him to take it. The monkey went at it
carelessly and was caught in the snare. When he accused the
fox of laying a trap for him, the fox replied: "O monkey,
fancy a fool like you being king of the animals!" In this way
those attempting things without due consideration not only suffer
for it, but also get laughed at!

[From the Greek of fable no. 38, p. 20, in Esope, *Fables*, ed. Emile Chambry
(Paris, 1967)]

The so-called epimythion, the moral taken from it, is wanting
in its Manichaean form but no doubt the Manichaeans found it a
useful appeal to be careful in one's actions especially as far as the
Divine Light is concerned:

"Who will now be the right king for us? There is none better
than you! All animals have approved Your Excellency as
absolute king and are at the point of declaring you king.
For Your Excellency's body is half like a man's, and half like
an animal's. Let us now go quickly, and you shall seat yourself
on the throne and be king over the animals!"

The foolish monkey got up and went along with the fox. When

they approached the [trap?] ,the [fox] turned back and spoke thus to the [monkey]: "Good ... has come before us and you have been placed before a good thing. Filled ... you would not ... the frame (?, the piece of meat?), but it is all presented and ready prepared for Your Excellency so that you shall eat well like a king. So if you will now take the trouble, take this frame (?) into your hands!"
The foolish monkey heard these words, at once he became very glad...

[T I, Sogdian: W.B. Henning, "Sogdian Tales," *BSOAS* 11 (1945): 474-75]

Another inexhaustible source from which the Manichaeans drew with joy and made known to others, was the *Panchatantra*, the origin of which, both geographically as well as chronologically, is unfortunately unknown. Certain, at any rate, is that it came out as a mirror for princes with the practical purpose of teaching the worldly wisdom (*artha, nīti*) that, together with religion and ethics (*dharma*) and love (*kāma*), was regarded as the object of all human longing. In the sixth century this collection, under the title of *Karatak ut Damanaka*, after two jackals (Sanskrit *Karataka* and *Damanaka*) that played a great part in the tales, was translated into Middle Persian by Burzōi, the physician-in-ordinary of the Sasanian king Khusrau Anōshirvān. Although this translation has been lost, it had time enough to make the basis of all later, still known translations, most of which also took over the Middle Persian title (but now as *Kalila*, the letters *r* and *l* being written in the same way, *and Dimna*, with loss of the final consonant).[35] Burzōi's text was, even before his death, translated into Syriac by a certain Būd, but Ibnu'l-Muqaffa's Arabic translation of it (eighth century) provided for the European diffusion of the tales. About A.D. 1200 they were translated into Hebrew by Rabbi Joel, otherwise unknown, and from there, about 1270, into Latin by Johannes de Capua as *Directorium Vitae Humanae alias Parabolae Antiquorum Sapientum*,[36] that formed the basis of all further translations into European languages.

All these translations, with the exception of the old Syriac one, have adopted the special introduction that Burzōi composed for his Middle Persian version and the genuineness of which, at least as regards the "new" tales given there, is undisputed. One of these tales, the origin of which thus in all probability is Iranian, is known from two Sogdian manuscripts. It is the tale of the pearl-borer:

... there was a quarrel, it could not be settled. So on the next day they went before a judge for a trial. The owner (viz. of the pearls) spoke thus: "My lord, I hired this man for one day, at a hundred gold dēnārs, that he should bore my pearls. He has not bored any pearls, but now demands his wages from me." The workman, in rebuttal, addressed the judge thus: "My lord, when this gentleman saw me at the side of the bazaar, he asked me: 'Hey, what work can you do?' I replied: 'Sir, whatever work you may order me (to do), I can do it all.' When he had taken me to his house, he ordered me to play on the lute. Until nightfall I played on the lute at the owner's bidding." The judge pronounced this verdict: "You hired this man to do work (for you), so why did you not order him to bore the pearls? Why did you bid him play on the lute instead? The man's wages will have to be paid in full. If again there should be any pearls to be bored, give him another hundred gold dēnārs, and he shall then bore your pearls on another day."

Thus under constraint, the owner of the pearls paid the hundred gold dēnārs; his pearls remained unbored, left for another day; and he himself was filled with shame and contrition.

The wise give this allegorical explanation: that man who understood all arts and crafts, represents [the body]... The pearl-borer is the body. The hundred [gold] dēnārs represents a life of a hundred years. The owner of the pearls is the soul, and the boring (?) of the pearls represents piety.

[T I TM 418 (Sogdian script) and M 135 (Manichaean script), Sogdian: W.B. Henning, ibid. p. 466 ff.; *Cat*. p. 11]

The allegorical explanation, in beautiful harmony with Manichaean practice, which has been given to the tale in both manuscripts, is quite different from the moral drawn by Burzōi. It consequently proves that the Manichaeans indeed reproduced the material borrowed but at the same time took the right to fix its educational applicability themselves. Another Manichaean example is The Three Fishes, a fable not to be found in Burzōi and accordingly neither in Ibnu'l-Muqaffaʿ, who, by the way, was called "the accursed heretic" by his opponents, nor in the European translations, but only in the genuine Indian tradition (V, 4).[37] It is rendered in a most concentrated form by the Sogdian text, almost like a paraphrase, but nevertheless it offers, together with the tale of the pearl-borer, convincing evidence of the Manichaeans' knowledge, use, and spreading of these tales in both their specifically western (Persian) as well as their specifically eastern (Indian) form:

> There was a big pond, and in it there were three fishes. The first fish was One-Thought, the second fish was Hundred-Thoughts, and the third fish was Thousand-Thoughts. At some time a fisherman came and cast his net. He caught those two fishes of many thoughts, but he did not catch the fish One-Thought.

[M 127, Sogdian: W.B. Henning, ibid., p. 471; *Cat.* p. 11]

V. Science and Magic

Still it seems obvious to ask why the success of Manichaeism was so colossal, why it was so attractive to people. No doubt the intrinsic details of Mani's teaching were never made by the pious Manichaean the object of a close scrutiny. They only established for him, in the myth (see p. 113 ff.) for example, the fact that, and the reason why, Evil existed; and beyond that they were of no practical importance. Thus the Roman Manichaean Faustus, St. Augustine's great opponent, does not discuss them. Rather, he seems to have considered them an obstacle to the mission in intellectual circles, an obstacle which might be neglected without pangs of conscience. There were other things, in addition to the myths that had a fascination for the people of the time. For some people it was without doubt, the interest of the Manichaeans in astronomy and other sciences, which can be dated back to Mani himself and must have been a prevalent motive for adopting the religion. But this interest, and hence the power really to offer a rational explanation of many of the problems to be tackled, varied greatly in intensity and range, depending on the individual personality. Beside the true scientist was the smatterer. The high Manichaean clergyman who in 719 was sent from Bactria to the Chinese Emperor, was in a class by himself. It can hardly have been Manichaeans of his kind who attracted the Barsymes mentioned in Procopius,[38] who took a great interest in "sorcerers and evil spirits" and was highly "fascinated by the so-called Manichaeans." And his approach certainly, would not have been in vain. The quite numerous Manichaean astrological and magical texts speak so as to leave no room for doubt:

Manichaean Magical Texts
a) A spell against fever

... Spell against fever and the Spirit of [Fever?]. And it is called Idrā. It has three forms and wings like a griffin. And it settles in the ... and in the brain (?) of men. And (then) it is called Fever. ... It is born in water ... and ashes ... thus ... [if the spirit of fever] does not go [of its own accord], then it shall come out [of the body] of NN. son of NN. and vanish in the name of the Lord Jesus the Friend, in the name of his Father the Highest, in the name of the Holy Ghost, in the name of the First Reflexion (*i.e.*, Ohrmizd, the Fisrt Man), in the name of Holy Êl, in the name of Baubo (?), in the name of Mūmīn the son of Êrich (?), (in the name of) Michael, Raphael, and Gabriel, in the name of ... the glutton, [in the name of] Sabaoth and ... Frēdōn shall throw down... all. And three forms are in me, and a belly(?) of fire. And in my hands I hold a sharp and stirring hatchet; I am girt with whetted sword and dagger of pure adamant, and have with me the whip of speech and hearing of the angels. ... The seven daggers (of) hard steel that I have grasped with my hand ... in great ... the hard ones ... all the ... of the house, and all the occult things of the house and all the evil spirits of the house and all the wrathful "robbers" of the house: I shall smite them and their downtrodden underfoot slaves so that they will not take up arms and stand against me. And I shall take away their light and add it to my brightness, and I shall take away their strength and add it to my own strength. And death that strikes ... is watching for them (?)...

[M 781, Middle Persian: W.B. Henning, "Two Manichaean Magical Texts," *BSOAS* 12 (1947): 40 f. *Cat.* p. 52]

b) From a Parthian amulet

... in your name, by your will, at your command, and through your power, Lord Jesus Christ. In the name of Mar Mani the Saviour, the Apostle of the Gods, and in the name of your Holy, praised, blessed Spirit, who smites all demons and powers of darkness. In the name of Michael, Sera'el, Raphael, and Gabriel ... of Qaftinus and Bar-Simus the angel ... in the name of An-el and Dal-el, Abar-el, Nisad-el, and Raf-el [who will smite] all you demons, yakshas,[39] peris, drujs, rākshasas,[40] idols of darkness, and spirits of evil. All ye sons of darkness and night, fear and terror, pain and sickness, ... and old age: from before the firm Power and Word ... away from this man, who wears it: flee ye, ... vanish, take flight, pass away until ... to a far place...

[M 1202, Parthian: W.B. Henning, ibid., p. 50 f.; *Cat.* p. 68]

To Augustine, on the other hand, the great disappointment was just that the scientific explanation he had expected in the great majority of cases proved to be pseudo-scientific. The majority of the people who became Hearers in spite of persecutions, however, sought something other than a scientific explanation of the phenomena of this world. They sought a redemption from the world and its malice. In Manichaeism they found a religion which could show them the way; Mani's gnostic religion could impart redeeming knowledge to them, theoretically and — much more important — practically.

VI. The Divine Light

Although the Manichaean aptitude for adaptation was taken quite far, particularly in terminology, Mani's actual message on the soul's tribulations and its hope of redemption did not suffer. Manichaeism was a soul service concentrating wholly and entirely on the salvation of the soul — that is, God's salvation and, because the soul was part of the divine life, simultaneously, man's salvation, for which his possession of a portion of Light was a requisite. In the western tradition, the sum of all the parts of Light in the chains of matter is called *Jesus patibilis*, "the suffering Jesus," known from Augustine (*Contra Faustum* XX, 2); because the life of Jesus, in the Manichaean interpretation, was one grand image of the tribulations of the divine Light in the material world. He himself, as representative of the Father of Light (see p. 113), brought to "the first man (Adam) wisdom and knowledge (that is, of his origin in the world of the light)" (quotation from a Middle-Persian text). The expression was relevant; because a correct understanding of Christianity, according to the Manichaean concept, was first given by Mani, whose account was precisely "as Jesus had preached" (quotation from the great Islamic geographer and historian *Birūni*, 973-1048). The significance of Jesus in this interpretation was so enormous that, contrary to the usual attempts at adaptation used in missionary technique, he was introduced by name in innumerable Central Asian texts. The actual espression *Jesus patibilis*, however, appears to have been restricted in location to North Africa, in the same way, as its precise plagiarism *Buddhagotra* (from Sanskrit *gotra*, "house, family, kindred, descendants") was to Buddhist regions. The name common to western and eastern Manichaeism given to the Light suffering in this world is the "Living Soul (Self)"—*viva anima* in Augustine — a designation which can be traced back to 1 *Corinth.* 15, 45: "The first man, Adam, became a living soul."

On the Living Self
You (i.e., the Elect) shall find eternal life; purify the Light Soul (Self) that it, for its part, may redeem you. Sing the

wonderful hymn: "In Grace, Peace and Confidence." Sing
out beautifully and gladly: "The Light-lute (?) of the souls."
Blow the trumpet which makes glad: "Gather the souls for
salvation." Gently come the sons of God at the voice of this
delightful song. Say: "Holy, Holy," call out: "Amen, Amen!"
Ring out: "The Light Wisdom," speak the pure talk: "The
Life-Word of Truth Sets Loose the Bound One from his Bond."
... Prepare the soul for purification and keep in holiness this
true secret. Honor those who will be saved, and teach them
this secret...

If you wish, I will instruct you from the testimony of the
fathers of old. The righteous Zarathustra, the saviour, when
talking with his soul (self), (said): "Deep is the drunkenness in
which you sleep; awake and look at me! Grace upon you from
the world of peace, whence I am sent for your sake." And it
answered: "I, I am the tender innocent son of Srōshāv (in
Parthian texts, a name borrowed from Zoroastrianism, of the
Father of Greatness), I am in the state of mixture (i.e., this
material world) and see suffering; lead me out from the embrace
of death." With "grace" Zarathustra asked of it: "(Are you)
the Word of Old, my member? The power of the living and
the peace of the highest worlds (come) upon you from your
own home. Follow me, son of gentleness (i.e., son of the First
Man), set the crown of Light upon your head (i.e., be redeemed)! You son of mighty ones that have become (so) poor that
you even have to beg at every place."

· · · · · · · · · · · · · · · · · · · ·

Teach the mixing of the pious and the sinful reflection and
separate one from the other. Understand your seed: the pure
Word that (in) itself is the pilot for the soul in the body. And
through it (the pure Word), fully know the false word that
leads to the hell of darkness, (is) a pilot of hell. Like a judge
weigh with the scales those redeemed and those condemned
by the Word. Remember the rebirth and the hard hell, where
the souls are oppressed and wounded in anguish. Keep the
zeal of the soul, the treasure of the Word that you may run to...

· · · · · · · · · · · · · · · · · · · ·

To you I will sing, skilled god, Living Self (Soul), gift from the
Father. You be blessed, Light Self, blessed, come in peace to
your home... O beneficent Mar Mani, we will always praise
his divine glory that showed you, Light Self, the escape...
I am from the Light and from the gods, and I have become
an exile, away from them. The enemies fell over me and have led
me to the dead. Blessed be — that he be saved — the one who

will save my soul (self) from distress. I am a god, born by the gods, brilliant, flashing ,and bright, shining, sweet-scented, and lovely, but now I have come into misery. I was seized by numberless disgusting demons of wrath who made me their prisoner. They humiliated me, bit me, tore me to pieces, and ate me. Demons, yakshas (imps), and witches, dark dragons difficult to avert, ugly, stinking, and black — from them I saw much pain and death. All cry out upon me and attack, pursue, rise against me...

[From M 7, Parthian: *MM* III: 870-75; *Cāt.* p. 2]

We pay homage to your glory, homage to Mar Mani who taught this secret in truth.

To you I will speak, my captive soul (self), remember your (real) home. ... Remember the devouring ... that bit you asunder and devoured you in hunger. ... Remember the hard battle of old and the many wars you had with the Powers (?) of Darkness. ... Remember the trembling, the weeping, and the grief that you had at that time, when the Father (i.e., the First Man) went up on high. Remember the middle line of the frontier and boundary of the two powers. ... Look at the mighty divine shape of the beloved fathers. Divine nature the beneficent, the reightreous believers, the glad Hearers will find; the divine palace those doing good will find...

[He (i.e., the First Man) was the son] of the Primeval Father and a prince, son of a king. He gave his soul (self) to the enemies, his whole dominion into fetters. All the Aeons and Domains (i.e., the Realm of Light) were afflicted for his sake. He prayed to the Mother of the Living, and she implored the Father of Greatness: "The beautiful son, the innocent, wherefore do the demons bite him asunder? ... collect your members (i.e., the dispersed Elements of Light)!" The eternally beautiful one, of bright shape, went up to his own march. The Mother welcomed and kissed him, saying: "You have come again, exiled son. Hurry and go into the Light, for those of your own stock are greatly longing for you."

[From M 33, Parthian: *MM* III: 875-77; *Cat.* p. 4]

The Divine Light is to be found not only in man and animals, but also in plants, particularly large fruitage such as cucumbers and melons, where the upward-striving light is gathered. A systematic release of all this light was effected by a daily meal at "the table", a cult action of sacremental character and no doubt inspired by the Christian's Eucharist. At this meal, the "chosen" (the Elect) ate the fruit brought by the "Hearers" (*auditores*) and absorbed the light to secure its safe return to the Realm of Light. In this way, those eating assumed a tremendous responsibility, since the light was of course part of divine life. With biting irony, Augustine speaks (in *De moribus manichaeorum* 39) of those Manichaeans who thought they could find God "with their nose and their palate." To the followers of Mani, however, the meal was a very serious matter indeed and a burdensome addition to religious responsibility. Not only their own personal redemption but also God's was entirely dependent upon the individual's ethical behavior. If the moral code was allowed to lapse or was breached, God was directly affected. Every sin was blasphemy. Against this background it can be appreciated that the Manichaean attitude to sin was terrifyingly serious, and they never — not even the holders of the highest religious offices — excluded the possibility of sin and damnation. Sin against the Living Self was fundamentally unforgivable:

> And the man (i.e., the Hearer) who is in the *Dēnāvariyya* (i.e., the eastern Manichaean church, see p. 18) should know how the service that he performs for the pure Elect ultimately [accrues?] to the soul; and should understand the fruits that are born out of the gifts. Then, even if his whole house were of gold and pearls and he gave it (to the Church) for the sake of the soul, he would not necessarily receive forgiveness. And [if it were] so that he could [bake] the flesh that is on his body into bread and would [cut] it with his own hand and give it to the Elect, ... he should know ... what ... [he who] would take *alms-food as(much as) a big mountain and could redeem it, should eat it. He himself will be saved, he will also save him who gave him the *alms-food, and it (i.e., the Living Soul (Self)) will reach the dome of the gods unharmed. And he who would take *alms-food as much as a single *grain of mustard but could not redeem it, then ... better for him ... fire ... who will find his seed-grain multiplied a thousand-fold.

> And the man who breaks faith with the Buddha and Apostle and leaves the Church and violates the commandments will be led, in great shame and fear, before the Just Judge, and he [cannot] turn [aside]. To him [the Judge will say:] you are ... the word ... to eat his body. And time and again they cut off his ears, and time and again they hack his tongue (?) into *slices, and in the same manner they cut all his limbs. And time and again they pour molten copper into his mouth and give him glowing-hot iron to eat and drive iron nails into his ears.

Who can wholly describe the wicked, horrible distress and suffering which that unfortunate unbeliever who soils the Pure Religion must undergo? Fortunate is the man that can completely keep ... the Pure Religion and the commandments ... because not ... not ever ... he does meritable works ... lust...

[T II D 162 I = 6020 I, Parthian: W.B. Henning, "A Grain of Mustard," *Annali Ist. Or. Napoli, Sez. Ling.* 6 (1965): 29 f.; *Cat.* p. 118]

This rigorous view of sin and its consequences is characteristic of Manichaeism and gives it its distinctive stamp, not only within the gnostic systems but also in the whole history of religion. The concept of God stands in near relation to the concept of sin. These reflections, closely following the strict paths of logic, must necessarily lead to a representation of the Manichaean god as *salvandus*, "one who is to be redeemed" — while there is still ravished light in the world — and becomes *salvatus* — "one who has been (finally) redeemed" — only when all light is liberated and the material world destroyed. On the basis of such considerations, it appears to be more justifiable to speak, not of god or deity, but of *the* divine, since everything divine is in Manichaeism a coherent whole. In its myth complex, several god-figures occur; but viewed in the greatest depth they are all identical with the Father of Light, from whom they emanate and who, more adequately expressed, is all that is divine. The question is, however, how was the individual Manichaean able, in the fervour of faith, to relate to such an abstract concept of God. The probable answer is that he adhered to the religion's theory, while in practice he created for himself a concrete concept of God, a god with whom he could establish a personal relationship. This is shown by the many beautiful hymns and prayers filled with religious sincerity, and the circumstance that Mani himself, at an early stage in the religion's history, was looked upon as a god, the redeemer. Similarly Buddha, the man who did not find room for any god in his teaching, nevertheless very soon — in Mahāyāna Buddhism — was considered to be a god himself, when implored by pious believers:

The father of our souls, divine Mani Buddha

[From an Uighur text, *APAW*, 1922, No. 2, p. 15]

Our highest god

[From an Uighur text, *SPAW*, 1930, pp. 200-201]

Mani, son of gods, Lord,
Vivifier, great ... of the religion, to you,
Chosen One, I pay homage.
May you be merciful, Father,
Mani, Lord, Life-giver.
He vivifies the dead
and brings light to those in darkness.
Make me go upwards, Mani, Lord ...

[From M 311 Middle Persian/Parthian: *HR* II: 66-67; *Cat.* p. 22]

Praise of the Apostle of Light.

(Behold), the illuminator of the hearts (comes), the lamp of
Light that even brightens those in darkness. Behold, the true
upraiser of the dead comes, who heals the illness...
Behold, the good and fortunate helmsman comes, who even
leads the ships out of the ... Behold, he comes ... (Behold, he
comes), the wise king of the beings of Light, who apportions
the good gifts. Behold, the ruiner of the enemies comes, who
destroys and disperses them. You, Father, Lord Mani, are
worthy of praise and blessing, and the gods and the Elements
of Light...

[M 224 I, Middle Persian: *MM* II: 322; *Cat.* p. 16]

You I will bless, God (*yazd*) Lord Mani.
Lord Mani I will praise.
O merciful God Lord Mani!
Turn to me and save me from ...
Turn to me, God (*bag*) Lord Mani.
O Illuminator, God (*bag*) Lord Mani.

[M 1, Parthian: F.W.K. Müller, "Ein Doppelblatt aus einem manichäischen Hymnenbuch (Maḥrnâmag)," *APAW*, 1912, pp. 20 ff., 26; *Cat.* p. 1]

From the Gods has come Lord (Mani),
the god with the dear name, to
paradise he leads up,
where the wind sweet
scent brings forth.
God, the Just One, has come from

the Paradise of Light.
the Helpful One, the truly Powerful One.

[M 64, Parthian: *HR* II: 92-93; *Cat.* p. 6]

And in a Parthian unpublished text (M 284, *Cat.* p. 20) containing Monday hymns
Have mercy on me, Jesus,
is paralleled to
Have mercy on me, God *(yazd)* Mani.
No wonder that the Apostle to his devoted followers was
Most beloved Mani

(from the Parthian M 338, ed. W. Sundermann, line 2109; *Cat.* p. 23), and no wonder that the Apostle's death was a terribly sad blow to all his communities.

VII. Mani's Death

Mani died during the reign of Shāhpuhr's second son Bahrām I (274-277), probably 277, when conditions had changed radically for the worse. After 26 days imprisonment he died in chains. In the pious tradition of the community, however, his death is referred to as his crucifixion, in conscious imitation of the story of Jesus' passion. This, therefore, is yet another example of Jesus' great importance in the Manichaean system. If Jesus, as the most typical gnosis-bringer, suffered death upon the cross in his phantom body (according to the Manichaean docetic view), Mani, as the last consummating redeemer-figure to follow him, had to suffer the same fate. A Middle Persian text provides a telling account of the atmosphere of coldness and reluctance in which he met the King of Kings:

> [Mani] ... came (viz., to the audience of Bahrām I), after he [had summoned] me, Nūhzādag the interpreter, Kushtai the [scribe?], and Abzakhyā the Persian. The king was at his dinner-table and had not yet washed his hands (i.e., he had not yet finished his meal). The courtiers entered and said: "Mani has come and is standing at the door." And the king sent the Lord the message: "Wait a moment until I can come to you myself." And the Lord again sat down to one side of the guard (and waited there)
>
> until the king should have finished his meal, when he was to go hunting. And he stood up from his meal; and, putting one arm round the queen of the Sakas and the other round Kardēr, the son of Ardavān, he came to the Lord. And his first words to the Lord were: "You are not welcome." And the Lord replied: "Why? What wrong have I done?' The King said: " I have sworn an oath not to let you come to this land!" And in anger he spoke thus to the Lord: "Ah, what need of you, since you go neither fighting nor hunting? But perhaps you are needed for this doctoring and this physicking? And you don't do even that!" And the Lord replied thus: "I have done you no evil. Always I have done good to you and your family. And many and numerous were your servants whom I have [freed] of demons and witches. And many were those whom I have caused to rise from their illness. And many

were those from whom I have averted the numerous kinds of
fever. And many were those who came unto death, and I have
[revived] them..."

[M 3, Middle Persian: W.B. Henning, "Mani's Last Journey," *BSOAS* 10
(1942): 949-52; *Cat.* p. 2]

Patēg (Pattikius), no doubt Mani's father, has related the events
leading up to his imprisonment, "at that time when the Pious
One (i.e., Mani) left the city of Ctesiphon" (*BSOAS* 10 (1942):
943; M. 6033, Parthian; *Cat.* p. 119):

Furthermore, Patēg saw another sign and spoke (thus): I see
that the Pious One has got up and for several days the Tigris ...
garment ... great ... held ... that majestically he enters and
leaves the wide royal (?) gate. Thereupon Kardēr the *Mōbad*[41]
planned with his friends who served before the king, and ...
jealous and cunning...

[T II D 163 = M 6031, Parthian: W.B. Henning, *ibid.* pp. 948-49; *Cat.*
p. 118]

There is also a relation of the very events connected with Mani's
death:

... because of ... together ... with hymns ... preaching and purification of the Living Self ... may you, one by one, teach help
to the Religion. And do not be slack in bearing the toil of the
Lord, so that you may find pious reward and retribution and
eternal life in the Highest." Then he (i.e., Mani) commanded
the *Epistle of the Seal* (see p. 60) of ... teaching ... he sent through
Mar Ammō the teacher to the whole Religion (i.e., the whole
Manichaean community). And all his children, the Elect and
the Hearers, paid homage to the Pious Lord (i.e., Mani),
and the Lord of Light (i.e., Mani) blessed all (of them) at
parting; and, weeping, they went away from him. And Uzzi
the teacher and two Elect [stayed] behind. And after ...

[M 454 I, Middle Persian: *MM* III: 891-92; *Cat.* p. 29]

Another prose text on Mani's death:

Just like a sovereign who takes off armour and garment and
puts on another royal garment, thus the Apostle of Light took
off the warlike dress of the body and sat down in a ship of Light
and received the divine garment, the diadem of Light, and the
beautiful garland. And in great joy he flew together with the
Light Gods that are going to the right and to the left (of him),
with harp (-sound) and song of joy, in divine miraculous power,

like a swift lightning and a shooting star, to the Column of
Glory, the path of the Light ,and the Moon-Chariot, the
meeting-place of the Gods. And he stayed (there) with God
Ohrmizd the Father.

And he left the whole herd of Righteousness (i.e., the Mani-
chaean Religion) orphaned and sad, because the Master of the
House had entered *Parinirvāna* (i.e., had died), and his house ...
Parinirvāna (?) ... and (it was under) the rulership of ... sing of the
zodiac, on the fourth of the month of Shahrevar, on the day of
Shahrevar, Monday and at the eleventh hour, in the province
of Khuzistān and in the city of Belabad, when this Father of
Light, full of power, was taken up to his own home of Light.
And after the *Parinirvāna* of the Apostle, Uzzi the teacher gave
this testimony to the whole Religion concerning what he saw
in the cohort, for that reason that he, Uzzi, that Saturday
night was left there with the Apostle of Light. And many pious
commands from the Apostle of Light he brought, orally, to
the whole Religion. And after the *Parinirvāna* of the Apostle
of Light, then (his) *Gospel,* the *Ardahang* and (his) garment and
hand(s) (i.e., the relics) ... the province ... Sisin (?) ...

[T II D 79 = M 5569, Parthian: *MM* III: 860-62; *Cat.* p. 111]

[In the year fifty-] five after the *Parinirvāna* of Mar Mani the
Apostle, when he rose up into the Moon-Chariot (and) stayed
with the Father God Ohrmizd, we will bless the Redeemer
Mar Mani.

[From T III D III 267 = M 8171, Parthian: *MM* III: 868-69; *Cat.* p. 134]

A hymn on the death of Mani can also be included:

The ever Powerful One stood in prayer, he implored the
Father with praise: "I have cleaned the earth and spread
the seed, and the fruit full of life I have brought before you.
I have built a palace and a quiet monastery for your *Nous.*
And the Holy Spirit I have sown in a green flower-garden and
brought a delightful garland to you. Brilliant trees I have
made fruitful, and I showed the road (leading) to the sons on
high. I have entirely accomplished your pious order for the
sake of which I was sent to this world. Take me (then) to the
peace of salvation, where I shall not any longer see the figure
of the enemies, nor hear their tyrannic voice. This time (viz. in
distinction to the previous rebirths) give me the great garland
of victory."

The Righteous God (i.e., the Father of Light) heard (his)
imploring and sent out the Envoys and the Great Gifts (saying):

"Give instructions to your Elect (i.e., the community), and (then) you: hither, come up to the eternal dwelling-place!" On the fourth of the month of Shahrevar, on the Monday and at the eleventh hour, when he had prayed, he shed the wonted garment of the body. Like the swift lightning he gleamed; brighter than the light of the sun the chariot glittered; and the Envoys spoke up and saluted the Righteous God. The house of the sky broke down to the outside; the earth trembled; a mighty voice was heard; and people that saw this sign were confused and fell on their faces. It was a day of pain and a time full of sorrow, when the Apostle of Light went into *Parinirvāna* (i.e., died). He left the leaders that guard the Church, and gave parting words of blessing to the whole great herd.

The Noble Prince (i.e., Mani) has fulfilled his promise that he spoke to us: "For your sake I will wait above, in the chariot of water (i.e., the moon, his resting place until the final salvation of the world) and always send you help." Behold, as 110 years have been completed, since you, o God, went to the assembly of peace, the time has now come that you take up (viz. into paradise) (your) Righteousness (i.e., your community) and raise up this throne of yours (in) higher (regions) (viz. in the Eternal Paradise, after the end of this world). Bravely we will wait in patience, the true shepherds, the faithful Elect and the Hearers. We will keep in our memory the advice of the gods and ...

[M 5, Parthian: *MM* III: 863-65; *Cat.* p. 2]

One might ask what sort of a man, then, was this Mani? It seems impossible to give a just answer; but it is beyond doubt that he was a religious personality of outstanding qualities, able to inspire and to call forth great enthusiasm. A letter from Mani to Mar Ammō, although fictitious, a *pia fraus*, although made upon a Buddhist model, and although a rather poor piece of hagiography, might, after all, tell us something about the strong spititual power of this man of God:

And whoever strikes you, do not strike him again. And whoever hates you, do not hate him back. And whoever envies you, do not envy him again. And whoever brings forth anger towards you, always speak with kindness to him. And what you detest in another person, do not do that yourself. No, one has to endure insults and other abuses from people above oneself, from people equal to oneself and from people under oneself; because nobody shall in any way make waver the devout one *(dēnāvar)* of good endurance. And it is as if one threw flowers against an elephant, and these flowers cannot smash the elephant; and as if rain-drops fell upon a stone, and these raindrops cannot melt the stone. Just so, insults and other abuses shall not in any way be able to make waver the devout one of good endurance.

Now the devout one must consider himself as high as the Sumeru mountain,[42] and now the devout one must humiliate himself as...

Now the devout one must show himself like a disciple and now like a teacher, now like a servant and now like a lord. Likewise, in this time of sin, the pure devout one must sit down in pious meditation, and he should turn away from sin and increase what is pious, so that ...

And therefore I have spoken these words, in order that everyone may himself pay attention to them and carefully listen to them. [For everyone] who hears and believes them and keeps them in his head and is active in pious deeds shall find salvation from this birth-death (i.e., *Samsāra*, the circling on, the cycle of transmigration) and be saved from all sins. Because I, Mar Mani, and you, Mar Ammō, and all those people of old and also those fortunate ones that are (re)born in this time, and likewise also those that will be (re)born in future, shall be saved from this birth-death through this pure commandment and through this perfect wisdom, through this activity and (this) humility. Because in this birth-death there is nothing good except only the merit and the pious deeds that men having knowledge do. Those who follow me, Mar Mani, and hope in God Ohrmizd and want the pure and just Elect *(dēnāvars)* as leaders, they are the ones that are saved and find salvation from this birth-death and reach eternal redemption.

[T II D II 134 I = M 5815 I, Parthian: *MM* III: 854-57; *Cat.* p. 115]

VIII. Manichaean Community Life

In all its aspects the Manichaean community life had only this one cardinal point: to liberate the Light imprisoned in matter; and everything was judged from this point. An act promoting the process was good; an act obstructing it was bad. This was the only yardstick for the cult itself, as well as for its ethical foundation. Manichaean community life, indeed, was one single interchanging relationship between the Elect and the Hearers who, through their Soul Service, their alms, "the daily gift" (in Sogdian) to the Elect, enabled the latter to liberate the Light more effectively. But this service is also the condition for the Hearer's own redemption; for they will be redeemed and purified, "each of them according to his works, (depending on) how he offered (gifts) to the Church" (*Kephalaia* 230). In very exceptional cases the Hearer may be able to acquire such qualities that his whole conduct is the same as that of the Elect, so that he will be redeemed immediately after his death (see p. 34). As a rule, however, he is supposed to be purified through the transmigration of the souls which plays such an important part in the Manichaean system, and which Mani himself is supposed to have taken over, according to the Muslim scholar Biruni (973-1051), while in India. The Elect received the Hearers' daily gift at the "table," and it consisted primarily of fruit, in particular cucumbers and melons, which were generally believed to possess a great deal of Light (God). The meal, probably the only real sacramental element in Manichaeism ,was opened by the Elect with an "apology to the bread." A question like "Whose flesh and blood is this?" when receiving the daily gifts from God's table appears to reveal convincingly the influence of the Christian Lord's Supper, even if there can be no question at all of a direct copy. For the Manichaean meal was daily and its intentions were fundamentally different from the Christian holy meal. Augustine, for example, mentions sarcastically that it was folly to believe one could find God "with the nose and palate" (*De moribus manichaeorum* 39). As in the Manichaean view the meal was a divine act of liberation, it was of vital importance to ensure

that those who received the offerings were worthy tools, that is
Elect; because otherwise one would literally inflict an injury on
the Father of Greatness himself. This caution and exclusivity
provided their opponents with opportunities to accuse the Manichaeans repeatedly of cruelty and brutality, although similar
regulations are known also among the Jews and the Christians.

Apart from the daily meal there were hardly any sacramental
acts. Baptism as a sacrament would be inconceivable in Manichaeism. A religion which claimed the acquisition of redeeming
knowledge, gnosis, as the only basis of salvation, would characterize
baptism, a sin-obliterating act, as blasphemy, on which it would
be a disastrous error to pin one's faith. "The Manichaeans say it
is in all eternity superfluous" (Augustine, *Contra duas epistolas
Pelagianorum* 4: 4-5). When, therefore, the Manichaeans mention
baptism, it can only be for purposes of mission and then exclusively
in a figurative sense. Even the *Bēma* feast does not give a clear indica-
tion of sacramental elements. The institution of this feast, the central
ceremony of the Manichaean cult, the liturgy of which is preserved
in the Sogdian text T II D 123 (see below), with hymn headings in
Parthian and Middle Persian, and the cult implements of which
are shown in a miniature found in Turkestan, of course, in the
nature of things, falls after Mani's death, its condition. In the
cultic act Mani appears as the divinized prophet who has authority
to forgive the repentant person's sins. Following the Uighur confession mirror for Hearers (*Khvāstvānīft* XIV A), one was supposed
to confess to the Tängri Burkhan (the "Divine Buddha" = Mani)
one's sins of the whole year and to ask for forgiveness. After that
the Seal Letter was read out whose precise contents are not known
but which was probably a last message from the jailed Mani.
Mystically and symbolically he is present, sitting on the throne
and judgment seat, *bēma*. "The doctor has come" *(af-ī)*, as it says
in the Coptic psalm-book, no doubt a rendering and interpretation
of the cultic shout *maranatha* of the primitive Church (cf. 1 *Cor.*
16, 22). Some description of the feast is given by Augustine in
Contra epistolam fundamenti VIII:

> At the time I was a Hearer among you I often asked why the
> Pascha of the Lord was generally kept with no solemnity at all,

or if at all, quite coldly and by only a few, with no vigil, with no lengthy fast enjoined upon the Hearers, with no festal array, while your Bema, that is the day on which Manichaeus (Mani) was killed, you marked with great honours the setting up of a platform approached by five steps, covered with precious hangings, an open object of adoration to all. When I asked the question, I say, the answer given me was that the day of his passion should be kept who had truly suffered; but as for Christ, seeing he was not born of woman, nor had presented to human eyes any true, but only a pretended flesh, he had not suffered, but feigned his passion.

Augustine's opinion that the Bema feast was celebrated *pro Pascha* is no doubt correct. There are several striking similarities between the two institutions: the very remembrance of a crucifixion (although the historical fact is that Mani's death was *not* a crucifixion), the congregational tradition of both, and the period of fasting prior to both the Bema feast and the Christian Easter Festival. It is, however, more important that *bēma*, word as well as object, is a loan from the Christian congregations, where it was known in all languages of the Church. In Armenian, *bem* was the sanctuary where the altar and the bishop's chair was placed, and in Greek, Syriac, and Coptic texts the word frequently occurs. [43]

There was a weekly confession of sins (Hearer to Elect, Elect to Elect) on Mondays (*Khvāstvānīft* XIII A) with a special liturgy and also with the singing of the so-called Monday hymns. A peculiar feature of the Manichaean cult was the body-soul rite whose contents and aim are, however, still obscure. Only a liturgical instruction and fragments of hymns relating to the celebration which went with this cult have been handed down. Funeral rites in the true sense were unknown in Manichaeism because death, which provided the opportunity to liberate a further part of Light, was regarded as good. Prayers to the dead, confirmed by literature, do not weaken this basic aspect. Following the Buddhist example, all practices of the eastern Manichaean Church were in particular linked with the *monasteries*. In the West, judging by the absence of testimony for the existence of these institutions, the cult was practiced during meetings in private houses or at a place chosen *ad hoc*. It is, however, immediately evident that the monasteries, as settled residences, influenced the Elect to a high degree in their pursuit of artistic activities and effectively demonstrated an educational value for the religion. Seen against this background, it is hardly surprising that Manichaean art developed far more freely and richly in Central Asia that it apparently did in the west, even if its high standard — especially in regard to book illuminations and calligraphy — was by no means unknown in the regions of its origin. The scribes formed a special class among the Elect. Since every Manichaean, Elect as well as Hearer, was an instrument for the liberation of the Light, he had to have certain ethical qualities. Both categories acquired and improved these qualities through the observance of certain regulations which were rigorously laid down for the Hearers in ten commandments and for the Elect in five commandments. elaborated with extreme vigour: 1) truthfulness, 2) non-injury (of the Light scattered over the whole world), 3) chastity, 4) purity of the mouth, and 5) living without personal possessions. For the Elect the Manichaean ethic was concentrated into the three seals, the seal of the mouth, of the hands, and of the bosom (*signaculum oris, manuum,* and *sinus* according to Augustine, *De moribus manichaeorum* 10-18).

Fasting, too, was a natural factor in the life of a Manichaean; but its terminology as well as its practice presents almost impenetrable difficulties. It was probably introduced by Mani himself without any particular guiding lines. It is certain that there was weekly fasting, on Sundays for the Hearers and on Mondays for the Elect; but Central Asian Manichaean texts indicate that fasting was also practised at other times and periods (e.g., the seven Yimkis and the month fast). However, the Manichaean's religious feeling, and fervour, as well as his intensive longing for redemption, is nowhere expressed more fully than in his prayers and hymns. There were daily prayers, seven for the Elect and four for the Hearers. The Manichaean's religious enthusiasm showed itself here in a much stronger form than one would have expected, judging from the abstract concept of God. There is some significance in Fortunatus' question whether Augustine knew something of the Manichaean world of prayers in addition to his theoretical knowledge (*Contra Fortunatum* 1). He would have been equally justified in pointing out the grandiose Manichaean hymn lyrics which

also took effect as complete cycles of which parts have been preserved (see p. 78 ff.).

Bēma Texts

Texts from the Parthian and Middle Persian part of M 801
(BBB). Its Sogdian part is a confession mirror for the Elect.

The Seal Letter

... (from) ... of the world and(from) Ammō, my most be[loved]
son and from all much beloved childern who are with me. To
all Shepherds, Teachers and Bishops, and to all Elect a[nd
Hearers], brothers and sisters, great and small, those of the
good soul that perfect themselves and are true, everyone who
has received this good message from me and who has become
contented with this teaching and pious action that I have
taught, and, without discord, is firm in the [b]e[lief]. To
everyone in person. (Sogdian:) The Seal Letter is finished.

Starting: Bēma hymns

[1] You we will praise, Mani the Lord. You we will praise,
Mani the Lord, king of the Holy Religion, most wise of the
great apostles. [2] We will praise your name, God, Lord Mani.
Make me happy, (you), loving vivifier of the dead. Give us
power and strength so that we can become perfect after your
command, God! [3] We will praise God Mani, the Lord.
We do reverence to your great brilliant glory. We honour the
Holy Ghost with the Glories and the mighty apostles.

[Bēma]Hymns

[4] Commander Maitreya Maitragar Maitr Chaitr, God Messiah, Mani'u Mani'i Mani'a Khaios, Vivifier, God Mar Mani.
[5] From paradise Mani has come! Rejoice, brothers! A light
day it has become to us, sons of the right hand. [6] From
paradise the gate was opened, and it was happiness to us:
the commander Maitreya has come, Mar Mani, to a new *Bēma*
(throne). [7] From the prosperous paradise the gate was opened
by the gods: garland, helmet, and diadem has appeared to us
all. ...

[Hymns] for the Bēma

[8] ... protect my body and save my soul; grant me (my) pious wish: the eternal Light-Paradise. [9] You we will laud, Jesus, you we will praise, Mani. The day became brightly shining, the day became brightly shining, Lord Mani of the noble name. [10] You we will praise, Light King, Son of Kings, Mani, the Lord, Mani, the Lord, Light King, worthy of praise.

[Bēma] Hymns

[11] You we will praise, Lord Mani, (and you) Jesus, Maiden (of Light) and Vahman and the beautiful *Bēma* and the apostles. [12] To you, Lord, I call, answer me, Lord; Mar Mani, Lord, forgive my sins, Lord. [13] Buddha Maitreya has come, Mar Mani, the apostle: he brought (our) victory from the righteous God (i.e., the Father of Greatness). To you, God, I pay homage, forgive my sins, save my soul, lead it up to the new paradise.

Praise of God Narisah (i.e., the Third Messenger)

... and the fortunate ancestors who are the light chariots, the brave hunters and the keen (?) helmsmen, the praised apostles, the great arrangers and the very strong powers, the spirits created by the (divine) word, the fortunate sovereigns, the light forms, the very best gods, the great saviours, the good helpers, the joy-giving deliverers, the keen (?) warriors and the strong battle-stirrers who have smitten death and conquered the enemies, and who have been led up in victory and arranged in peace: may they ever be praised through the praise of the light Aeons, and may they be praised through the strong praising of the Holy Religion so that their great peace, their pious protection and nourishing full of life can be arranged all over the Holy Religion, particularly over this place and (this) blessed assembly ...

[Praise of] Srōshahrāy (i.e., the Column of Glory)

... to all of us, the just believers and the meritorious Hearers. So (be it) for ever and ever! Blessed and praised be this mighty power, the light and beneficent God, the Perfect Man (i.e., the Column of Glory). House and covering for all souls, road and path for all lights and redeemed souls — may he be blessed so that his radiance of life may shine upon the Elect Religion and bring forth peace, health and confidence for us in all lands. And may he protect us for wonderful joy and accept from all of us this pure prayer, living voice and divine song. So (be it) for ever and ever!

Finished: the Srōshahrāy (Hymns). Six.

(Hymns) on Jesus the Vivifier have begun

Praised be the holy wisdom: Jesus the Splendour, the Maiden of Light and the Great Vahman (i.e., the *Nous*, the personification of the Manichaean religion), the brave saviours, the raisers of the dead of the Holy Religion. Praised be these great healers, healing the Highest Self so that they over us also may increase peace and health, joy and piety, salvation and the victory of the battle-stirrers and the mighty and make us worthy of the great glory and the eternal diadem. So be it in all future and for ever and ever. (Author) Kirbakkarzādag.

Blessed and praised be Jesus, the vivifier, the New Aeon, the true raiser of the dead who indeed is the mother giving life to those who have died from the wounds and lesion of Greed and Lust, and the healer to those who become unconscious through the illness of the body of death. And he saw for the blind, heard for the deaf ...

[Chants of Praise of the Apostles]

All the bishops, the house leaders (i.e., the presbyters), those, being in charge of the prayers, the wise preachers, the good scribes, the hymn singers with the melodious voice and all the pure and holy brothers: may they be remembered through pious action. The holy virgin sisters together with their assemblies and monasteries: may they be remembered through pious action. And all Hearers, brothers and sisters, from the east (and) the west, the north and the south who profess God, Light, Power and Wisdom: may they be remembered through pious action.

May praise, blessing, pleaing, prayer and imploring from us all ascend in purity and grace and be accepted by our beneficent fathers and adorable ancestors. And may they on their part send us power and help, salvation and v[ictory, he]alth and safety, joy and piety, peace and confidence, love (?) and protection, pious striving and perfecting and the forgiveness of sins, the true light of health. May (all that) be arranged over the whole Holy Religion, especially over this place and (this) blessed assembly, over me and you, dearest brothers, holy virgin sisters, Hearers of good soul. (All this) so that we may be protected and tended through the hand of the light apostles and the mighty church leaders. So be it in one living [and holy] name in the future and for ever and ever.

May the Living Self reach redemption, those rich in gifts be without sin, and all of us find salvation. So be it in one living and holy name in the future and for ever and ever...

. . . .

. . . .

The chants or praise of the throne (*Bēma*) have begun. We bend the knee in deep worship. We do reverence and praise to the powerful god, the praised king and adorable lord of the Light Aeons, according to whose wish and instigation you, our Highest God, have come to us. We do reverence to Jesus, the Lord, the Son of Greatness, who sent you, dearest one, to us. We do reverence to the praised Maiden, the Light Twin, who in every battle was your helper and companion. We do reverence to the Great Vahman, who was set by you in the heart of those of the good soul (i.e., the Hearers). We do reverence to your great glory, our father, apostle of light, Mani, the Lord. We do reverence to this noble throne (i.e., the *Bēma*) and (this) brillant seat on which you have sat down. We do reverence to the radiant diadem that you have put on your head. We do reverence to this noble form and beautiful picture. We do reverence to the Gods and apostles who have come with you. We do reverence to the whole Electness and (above all) your blessed deputy, Lord. We do reverence to the great teachers. We do reverence to the powerful bishops. We do reverence to the wise house-leaders. We do reverence to the good scribes. We do reverence to the hymn-singers with the melodious voice. We do reverence to the pure just (i.e., the Elect). We do reverence to the holy virgins (i.e., the female Elect). We reverence and praise the whole Herd of Light that you yourself have chosen through the spirit of truth. And from your glory, Lord, and from the glory of all these, I beg, as a (gift of) grace to all my limbs, that sense may enter my heart, reason my intellect, thought my mind and ...

The hymns of the joyful have begun

You are beaming, cheerful picture, like the sun, you leader of the truth, of the same form as God Zurvan (i.e., the Father of Greatness). On this day of joy our heart shall lighten you with its love: come in good health, the apostles shall give you peace.

For a new (lit. other) omen may that leader be blessed who has come to a mighty day of joy. May the gods give you peace, may the apostles protect you, and may Vahman send you new eternal life.

Melody: "Come for a New Good Sign." Come for a new good sign and a good omen and for days of everlasting joy to this assembly of gods and apostles! From all regions and many lands the Glories, Spirits and Light Gods have come together in joy on this day in order to receive you, Lord, leader of praised name, in love and to be your guardians against all enemies and injurers of the religion. With mighty joy we will reverence you and take great delight in your fortune. (Written by:) Istayidag...

Come, light-giving Sun, come, radiant full Moon, come, merciful Lord, strong and of great knowledge. Receive [ever] new blessing from Vahman, the king; be joyful and be happy in everlasting delight.

To (the tune of) "Lord Mani has come." The light-giving Sun came, shone, beamed in the heavens. Its light gleamed in all lands and regions. We, (the whole) brotherhood, are ready to do reverence to it that it may give us joy and eternal life. This (hymn) to the tune of: "You are the Mighty God." The giver of peace and health has come, the one who brings forth peace and health to the whole religion. Increase (this) peace and health for the flock, the assembly and the Elect! May peace and health come to you from the mighty and highest God; may Light, Power and Wisdom give you peace and health. Praised you are and shall (always) be by the Holy Religion. May the apostles, the Glories and the Spirits give you peace. Live in joy; be glad and happy in new peace; give light to the children through the spirit full of life. (Written by) Bay Aryaman.

This (hymn) in Sogdian mode. A new light-giving sun has come, and a new apostle, a man of teaching from the eastern region.

He has brought new joy and new confidence and new mighty progress to the whole Holy Religion. The apostles, the Glories, the Spirits rejoice in you, fortunate leader, head of the praised name. May you live in healthiness and new peace and in new ...

[From M 801, Parthian and Middle Persian: *BBB* v. 1-199, 218-67, 299-307, 310-67, and 390-475; *Cat.* p. 54]

From a Bēma Liturgy

... from paradise Mani, the Lord, wants to go. When you go, Lord, (then) save also us from birth-death! You go, Mani; save me, Commander Maitreya! (Twice) And later on: You we call, you noble commander with the beautiful name, Mar Mani. You, Bringer of Light, we praise loudly. And when the name of the souls is called, finish the hymn (and) stop a little. And then take ... from the *Evangel* and pay homage to the apostle and the just (i.e., the Elect). And the confession begins. And when it has come to an end, the three hymns (to be sung) are the following: Mar Mani, Noble Glory, Beautiful Sight. You, Father, I Implore: Forgive my Sins! Beneficent Mar Mani, oh God, Answer us! (Twice) Oh Mani, vivifier with the noble name, save me, save, forgive my sins! And when the words of the Seal Letter have been said (?), then, facing the Apostle, sing this hymn: My Light Father, Mar Mani, Ascended to Paradise. And after the Meal the three hymns (to be sung) are the following: Commander with the Beautiful Name, God Mar Mani Oh Lord, You Go Away, Lead Also Me Up to Paradise. A Messenger Came...

[T II D 123 = M 5779, Middle Persian, Parthian, Sogdian: *BBB* c, p. 45-46; *Cat.* p. 114]

From Monday Hymns

... in the Paradise of Light, the primeval home, I shall find joy with the Light Gods; and there I shall dwell for ever ... the New Man puts on the divine garment...

Have mercy [on] me, Second Greatness (i.e., the Third Messenger)! Have mercy on me, Perfect Man (i.e., the Column of Glory), Jesus and Maiden of Light! Have mercy on me, God Mar Mani!

[From M 284 a and b, Parthian: F.W.K. Müller, "Eine Hermas-Stelle in manichäischer Version, *SPAW*, 1905, p. 1082 f., R. Reitzenstein, "Das mandäische Buch des Herrn der Grösse und die Evangelienüberlieferung," *SHAW*, 1919, 12. Abh., p. 5 (F.W.K. Müller), W.-L. I, p. 61; *Cat.* p. 20]

The Uighur Khvāstvānīft in Translation

Khvāstvānīft, a Parthian word, is used as a name of a long confessional text primarily in Uighur (Old Turkish). It is laid down for the Hearers and is itself a translation from an Iranian original, which, apart from two Sogdian fragments, has been lost. Similar texts intended for the Elect are also known, again in Sogdian, most probably because they represented a genre unknown to the earliest Manichaean literature. In Middle Persian there is only one specimen of that kind (M 210, see below), a late Central Asian product. But the importance of these texts is evident. They reflect everyday life, picturing Manichaeism in general terms, its theology, ethics, in short, its very essence.

I B Khormuzta tängri (i.e., the First Man) came (and) descended together with the Fivefold God (i.e., the five Elements of Light) in order, at the command of all gods, to fight the devil. He fought Shimnu (i.e., Ahrmēn) with the evil deeds (and) with the five kinds of devils. Then God and devil, Light and Darkness were mixed. Khormuzta tängri's son, the Fivefold God, our soul, fought for some time against the devil (and) was wounded. And being mixed with the evil knowledge (or wickedness) of the uppermost one of all devils (and) of the insatiable and shameless Āz (Greed) devil's 140 myriads (or: Āz devil (and) the 140 myriads) of devils, he became witless and weak-willed. He completely forgot the land of the immortal gods, in which he himself was born and created, (and) parted from the gods of Light.

I C If from then on, my God, by the fact that Shimnu with the evil deeds by devilish action seduced our intellect and our thoughts, (and) because we (thus) [at last] had become without knowledge and intellect, we [somehow] should have sinned and erred against the holy (pure), light Äzrua tängri (i.e., the Father of Greatness), the origin and root of all souls of light, (and) have called him the origin and root of Light as well as Darkness (and) God as well as the Devil, if we should have said: "If anybody quickens, (it is) God, (who) quickens, if anybody slays, (it is) God, (who) slays," (or) if we should have said: "God (= Äzrua) has created the good and the evil entirely," if we should have said: "He (= Äzrua)is the one who has created the immortal gods," or we should have said: "Khormuzta tängri and Shimnu are brothers," ... if we, my God, ever, unwittingly false to God, should in this way have used great blasphemous speech (and) thus done sin bringing perdition, (then), my God, I repent, Raymast Frazend, now, praying to be delivered from sin. Forgive my sin! Blissful be[ginning]!

II A Secondly. Also (the sins) against the god of the sun and moon, against the gods sitting in the two palaces of Light (actually: camps of princes).

II B If one goes to the land of the gods, the origin, root, and rallying-ground of all prophets, the pure doctrine, the souls provided with good action (and) the Light belonging to the earth, the god of the sun and moon is its front door. In order to free the Fivefold God and separate Light and Darkness, they revolve in a circle (and) irradiate the four quarters (of the heavens).

II C My God, if we ever, unwittingly, should somehow have sinned against the god of the sun and moon, the gods who sit in the two palaces of Light, and if we should not have believed: "True, mighty, and powerful is the god (of the sun and moon)," if we should somehow have used much evil blasphemous speech, and if we should have said: "The sun and the moon will die (perish)," if we should have said: "Without (their own) power they rise (and) set. If their (own) power is present, (then) make them stop rising!" (and) if we should have said: "Our Self is different from the sun and the moon," (then) we pray, when we unwittingly have committed this other sin, to be forgiven (redeemed). Forgive my sin!

III A Thirdly. Likewise (the sins) against the Fivefold God, Khormuzta tängri's son.

III B Firstly, Zephyr tängri, secondly, Wind tängri, thirdly, Light tängri, fourthly, Water tängri, fifthly, Fire tängri. When he (i.e., the Five Elements together) for some time had fought the devil, (and) because he (in this connection) was wounded and mixed with Darkness, he could not go (return) to the land of gods (and therefore) is on this earth. The tenfold heaven above (and) the eightfold earth below (only) exist for the sake of the Fivefold God. Blessing and happiness, color and appearance, self and soul, power and light, (and) origin and root of everything on earth are the Fivefold God.

III C My God, if we ever somehow, unwittingly (or) by badness and wickdness should have broken or destroyed the Fivefold God, if we should have inflicted on him the fourteen-fold wounds, if we somehow with the ten serpent-headed fingers (and) the 32 teeth should have tortured and pained the Living Self, (viz.) the god of eating and drinking (the god, the divine of food and drink), (and) if we should somehow have sinned against the dry and wet earth, against the five kinds of living beings, against the five kinds of herbs and trees, (then) we now pray, my God, to be liberated from sin. Forgive my sin!

IV A Fourthly. (About sins) against the always existing messengers of God, the prophets.

IV B If we should somehow, unwittingly have sinned against the holy Elect, who do meritorious deeds, and bring redemption, and if we, although we called (them) "true messenger of God" and "prophet", (still) should not have believed (this): "The holy Elect is characterized by good deeds," (or) if we, when they proclaimed the law of God, (still) out of unwisdom should have opposed, (or) if we, not spreading the doctrine and the law, (on the contrary) should have obstructed them, (then), my God, we now repent (and) pray to be liberated from sin. Forgive my sin.

V A Fifthly. (About sins) against the five kinds of living beings.

V B And (that is) firstly, against the two-legged human beings, secondly, against the four-legged living beings, thirdly, against the flying living beings, fourthly, against the living beings in the water, (and) fifthly, the living beings creeping on the ground on their belly.

V C If we ever, my God, somehow should have inspired with fear (or) scared these five kinds of living beings from the biggest to the smallest, if we somehow should have beaten or cut them, somehow have pained and tortured them, (indeed,) somehow should have killed them, (then) we to the same degree owe life to the living beings. (Therefore) we now, my God, pray that we may be liberated from sin. Forgive my sin.

VI A Sixthly. Likewise, my God, if we ever in thought, word, and deed should have committed the ten kinds of sins:

VI B If we should somehow have been false and somehow committed perjury, if we should somehow have been witness for a false person, and if we should somehow have prosecuted an innocent person, and if we by spreading rumours should somehow by (our) words have exasperated a person (and thus) have corrupted his heart and mind, if we should somehow have practised black magic, and if we should somehow have killed many living beings, if we should somehow have cheated and deceived, if we should somehow have used a strange (another) person's goods (entrusted to our care), if we should somehow have performed an action of which the God of the Sun and Moon does not approve, and if we should somehow have sinned and erred with the first self (and) with this self, after we ourselves have become "long-mantled", if we should somehow have inflicted destruction and ruin on so many living beings, (then), my God, we now pray to be liberated from the ten kinds of sins. Forgive my sin.

VII A Seventhly. And if one should ever ask (lit. say): "Who (comes) to the road that seduces to the beginning of the two poison roads (and) to the gate of Hell" (then) it is in the first place the one who adheres to a false doctrine and law, (and) in the second place likewise the one who worships the devil and addresses him as God.

VII B If we, my God, should ever somehow, without recognizing and understanding the true God and the pure (sacred) doctrine (and) without believing, when the prophets, the pure (holy)

Elect preached, allowing ourselves to be deceived by one who falsely and mendaciously (lit. wrong and false) maintained (said): "I am a man of God and a preacher" (and) accepted his words, have fasted erroneously (erring), should somehow have worshipped erroneously, should somehow have given alms erroneously, and if we should somehow, erring, have performed an evil action, saying (at the same time): "We do meritorious deeds which bring redemption," and if we, when addressing the devil and the demon as "God," should have worshipped (them) by killing living beings and if we, saying: "(He is) a prophet," should have cherished a false doctrine (and) shown (it (the doctrine) or him (the "prophet")) worship and honour (and thus) sinning against God have served the devil, (then), my God, we now repent (and) pray to be liberated from sin. Forgive my sin.

VIII A Eighthly. (Ever) since we have recognized the true God (and) the pure (sacred) doctrine, we know "the two principles" (roots, origins) (and) "the doctrine of the three times". We know the light principle, the Realm of God, (and) the dark principle, the Realm of Hell. And we know what existed previously, when there was no earth and heaven, we know why God and the devil were fighting, how Light and Darkness were commingled, (and) who created earth and heaven, and finally we know why earth and heaven (once) will cease existing, how Light and Darkness will be separated, (and) what then will be (happen).

VIII B In Äzrua tängri, in the God of the Sun and Moon, in the powerful God and the prophets we have put our trust, we have relied on them (and) have become Hearers. Four Light seals have we sealed in our hearts: Firstly love, the seal of Äzrua tängri, secondly faith, the seal of the God of the Sun and Moon, thirdly the fear (of God), the seal of the Fivefold God, (and) fourthly wisdom, the seal of the prophets.

VIII C My God, if we should have let (have removed) our intellect and our heart get away from these four kinds of gods ("divine (aspects)," "this Fourfold God"), if we should have shaken (them) away from their (right) place, (and) if (thus) God's

seal should have been annihilated, (then) my God, we now
pray to be liberated from sin. Forgive my sin!

IX A Ninthly.(Ever) since we have obeyed the ten commandments,
it was necessary closely to obey three with the mouth, three
with heart, three with the hand, (and) one with the whole self.

IX B My God, if we should wittingly (or) unwittingly, as we lived
(went, walked) in love of ourselves (in selfishness) (or) caught
(accepted) a bad companion's and friend's word (and) saw
with his mind (heart)(or) troubled about cattle and property,
or our grief and our distress appeared (fell upon (us)), have
broken these ten commandments, (or) if we should somehow
have put up with defects and errors (viz. in the keeping of
these commandments), (then), my God, we now pray to be
liberated from sin. Forgive my sin!

X A Tenthly. There is a rule that one must every day direct four
acts of praise (prayers) to Äzrua tängri, to the God of the Sun
and Moon, to the powerful God, and to the prophets, in simplic-
ity (sincerity) and with a pure heart.

X B And if we, being negligent without having fear (of God),
should not have praised (prayed) correctly and completely and,
while praising (praying), not have kept our hearts and our
thoughts directed toward God, (and) our praise and our
prayer (thus) should not in purity have reached God, (or) if
somewhere there should have been something which obstructed
(or) impeded, (then), my God, we now pray to be liberated
from sin. Forgive my sin!

XI A Eleventhly. Likewise there is a rule, that one is to give the
pure (sacred) doctrine (religion) a sevenfold present. And if
the angels gathering the light of the Fivefold God (and) Khrōshtag and Padvākhtag tängri [44] should let the light of the Fivefold
God, which goes up to heaven and is liberated, come to us,
(then) there is a rule that we very excellently putting it in
order and arranging it, shall lead it to religion.

XI B If we, either because of distress, or being miserly about
giving alms, should not have been able to give the sevenfold
alms to its full extent to Religion, if we should have tied the
light of the Fivefold God, which goes up to Heaven and is

liberated, to house and property (or) have given it to a person of bad action (or) an evil being, (or) we should have shed it (or) thrown it away, (or) we should have sent God's light to an evil place, (then), my God, we now pray to be liberated from sin. Forgive my sin!

XII A Twelfthly. There is a rule that like the holy Elect one is in one year to celebrate wusantī (fast) for 50 days, (and) it is necessary to praise God (repay God) by observing the sacred (pure) fast.

XII B And if we, as we, in order to maintain house and property, worried about (were occupied by) cattle and goods, or because our need and our distress supervened, (or) still because of the insatiable and shameless Āz demon and our heart devoid of fear (of God), (or) as we were lazy and indolent (negligent), voluntarily (or) involuntarily should have broken the fast (or) further, while we were fasting, had not fasted correctly according to the religion and the doctrine, (then), my God, we now pray to be liberated from sin. Forgive my sin!

XIII A In the thirteenth place. It is necessary that every Monday we should pray to God, religion, (and) the holy (pure) Elect to forgive our errors and our sins.

XIII B And should we not, voluntarily (or) involuntarily, as we were lazy and indolent (negligent), (or) as we mentioned business (or another) undertaking as a pretext, have gone to obtain forgiveness for (be liberated from) sin, (then), my God, we now pray to be liberated from sin. Forgive my sin!

XIV A In the fourteenth place. There is a rule that in one year one is to celebrate seven *Yimki* (festivals), (and) we are in duty bound to obey the one month commandment (precept, viz. concerning fast). Likewise we are obliged, after celebrating the *Yimki* (festival), fasting, at the *Bēma* sincerely (lit. with an insight) (and) with all our hearts to pray to Tängri Burkhan (i.e., Mani) to forgive our sins through one year.

XIV B My God, if we should not have been able to celebrate the seven *Yimki* (festivals) completely (or) not been able correctly and completely to obey the commandment of a month('s fast) at all, and we should not at the *Bēma* have been able to celebrate the *Yimki* fast correctly according to the religion and the doctrine (or) sincerely (actually: with an insight) (and) with all our hearts have prayed (to Tängri Burkhan) to forgive our sins through a year, (indeed), if somehow there should have been error and defect, (then), my God, we now pray to be liberated from sin. Forgive my sin!

XV A In the fifteenth place. Every day we somehow are thinking bad thoughts, somehow speak sinful words which one should not speak (and) somehow do deeds which one should not do.

XV B Because of the evil deeds and sin we incur agony upon our-selves (our own selves), and the light of the Fivefold God, which we in the course of day (during the day) have eaten, goes to the evil place, because we ourselves, our souls, wandered (lived) in love of the insatiable and shameless Āz demon (actually: according to the... Āz demon's love). For this reason (because of this, therefore), my God, we pray to be liberated from sin. Forgive my sin! For the sake of the divine omen of religion!

XV C My God, we are encumbered with defect and sin, we are great debtors. Because of the insatiable and shameless Āz demon, we in thought, word, and deed, likewise looking with its (i.e., Āz's) eyes, hearing with its ears, speaking with its tongue, seizing with its hands, (and) walking with its feet, incur constant and permanent agony on the light of the Fivefold God in the dry and wet earth, the five kinds of living beings (and) the five kinds of herbs and trees. Likewise we (in other ways) are encum-bered with defect and sin: Because of (by) the ten command-ments, the seven alms, and the three seals we have name of Hearer (the Hearer's name), (but) we are unable to do his deeds.

If likewise we should somehow have sinned and erred against the gods of Light, the pure (sacred) doctrine (religion) (and) against the men of God and the preachers, the pure (holy) Elect, and if we should not have wandered (lived) in accordance with the doctrine and wisdom communicated (said, preached) by God, if we should have broken the hearts of the gods and been unable to celebrate *Yimki*, fast, prayer, and command-ments in accordance with religion and the doctrine, (and) if

we somehow should have put up with defects and errors. ..
every day, every month (indeed) we are sinning! ... (then) we
pray to the gods of Light, Nom qutī (i.e., Vahman, the personified church) (and) the pure (holy) Elect to be liberated from
sin. Forgive my sin!

Eleventh month, on the twenty-fifth day.

[T II D 178 IV, T II D III, the Stein text Ch. 0015 of the British Museum,
Uighur: Jes P. Asmussen, *X^uāstvānīft. Studies in Manichaeism* (Copenhagen,
1965) p. 167 ff.]

A Confessional Formulary for the Elect

Recto

(1) [great] and small (viz. commandments) and
(2) also the other injunctions and
(3) morals that are to the pure
(4) and perfecters
(5) prescribed I
(6) in them slack and
(7) deficient, weak and
(8) negligent am. However
(9) what can I
(10) say! In (right) thinking

Verso

(1) prayer and v[oice]
(2) to my own regions of
(3) Light address and
(4) the first and the last
(5) of this Living Self re-
(6) member? And by
(7) invocation in
(8) nights and days.
(9) vigilance, eagerness,
(10) attentive hearing as in ...

[M 210, Middle Persian: W.B. Henning, "Bráhman," *TPS*, 1944, p. 114,
Jes P. Asmussen, op. cit., p. 241; *Cat.* p. 15]

IX. Manichaean Hymn-Cycles

In the community life of the Manichaeans, hymns played an out-standing part. Through the beauty in art and poetry, skilfully depicted by their painters and poets, the mind was turned to the wonderful destination of the redeemed. It is quite understandable, therefore, that the bulk of Middle Persian and Parthian texts are hymns, many of which are "cantillated," made usable for chanting. Formally they can, according to Professor Mary Boyce (*HdO* IV,2, 1968, p. 74), be divided into three categories: the long hymn-cycies; the long but undivided chants of praise (Middle Persian *āfurishn*, Parthian *āfrīvan*); and the short hymns (Middle Persian *mahr*, Parthian *bāshāh*). The manuscript M 1 II from the eighth century is an index with the opening lines of hymns, of which a considerable number has been preserved elsewhere:

"We will bless and praise" (340)

"May we find mercy from you" (347)

"Show mercy to me, Great God" (352)

"May there be well-being, peace and happiness" (378)

"The blessed day of joy has come" (382)

"We will bless you, Light Self" (415)

"Come, brothers, let us sing" (425)

[From M 1 II, Parthian: F.W.K. Müller, *APAW*, 1912; *Cat.* p. 1]

In the extant Manichaean literature the long hymn-cycle is represented by two Middle Persian texts, *The Speech of the Living Self (Gōvishn īg grīv zīndag)* and *The Speech of the Light Self (Gōvishn īg grīv rōshn)*, and by two Parthian texts, *Fortunate for Us (Huvīdagmān)* and *Rich (Friend) of the Beings of Light (Angad Rōshnān (Friyānag)*, attributed to Ammō, the great missionary of the east. Fragments of a Sogdian translation of the Middle Persian as well as the Parthian texts are known, and a fragment of an Uighur Turkish translation of the *Huvīdagmān* has been published by W.B. Henning (*AM* n.s. 7 (1959): 123 f.).

The Middle Persian cycles are devoted to the Living Self,

the divine Light in the prison of matter, Augustine's Jesus *patibilis*, as holy as the sacred fire and water of the Zoroastrians. It suffers, being treated in many different ways, like a slave, like a lord, like a friend, like an enemy, etc. In this situation sin loiters everywhere, but by the help of the world of Light it is washed away, when the redeeming knowledge comes.

The Parthian texts tell about a soul in distress, surrounded by dangers from all sides, its fervent longing for salvation, the coming of the Saviour and hence the promise of being able to begin the journey to the New Paradise, the dwelling of the rescued souls until their return to the Eternal Paradise (the Real Paradise in a Sogdian text) at the final victory of Light. The *Huvidagmān* in addition has an opening canto describing paradise and a canto entitled "The Punishment of Sinners." It is difficult, from the material at hand, to determine the liturgical use of these texts, but probably we have to do with a death-mass of some kind.

From the Gōvishn ig grīv zindag

1

a

You buy me like slaves from thieves,
and you fear and implore me as (you do) lords.
Like disciples from the world you elect me (to be among) the
[righteous,
and you show me reverence as (you do) masters.
You smite and hurt me like enemies,
and you save and vivify me like friends.
However, my Fathers (i.e., the Light Gods) have power and might
to offer you thanks in many ways
And as a reward for one day of fasting,
to give you the eternal happiness.
And in order to send you the share that through me is yours
they will send the Gods before you.
And (also) the share in toil and worry (?)
that you bear and suffer for my sake.

b

I am the Fire which Zarathustra built up,

and he bade the righteous build me up.
Build me up ... do not make!
And do not ... to build up the ...
From the seven consecrated, sweet-smelling fires
bring me, the Fire, purified fuel.
Bring forth clean firewood,
and delicate and fragrant incense.
Kindle me with knowledge,
and give me clean offering!
I am the Water which (is) fit
that you should give me "the offering to the water" that I may
                                          [become strong.

[M 95, Middle Persian: *MM* II, pp. 318-20; *Cat.* p. 8. Cf. Mary Boyce,
"Ātaš-Zōhr and Āb-Zōhr," *JRAS*, 1966, p. 100 ff.]

2

And my body he (i.e., Jesus, the saviour) shall cure from pain,
and from being despised he shall make me adorable.
And he shall wash me (clean) from the dirt and the heavy
                                          [sinfulness,
and he shall bath me and lighten me.
And he is my great intermediator
and my protection and my true refuge.
He is the one who guides me away from all sins (?),
and who frees me from ...
He is the one who saves me from trouble (?)...

[M 564, Middle Persian: *MM* II: 321; *Cat.* p. 40]

3

And he shall wash me (i.e., the Soul) with a laving ...
that is from the land of high ...
And he shall raise me on wings of ...
upwards to the dwellings of ...
And shall set (?) me in the treasure-house of the Father,
where no thieves shall loiter...

[M 570, Middle Persian: W.B. Henning, "A Farewell to the Khagan of
the Aq-Aqatärän," *BSOAS* 14 (1952): 516; *Cat.* p. 40]

From the Parthian Hymn-Cycles
Huvīdagmān
Canto I

(1) (It was) fortunate for us that through you we knew and
[accepted your teaching.
Beneficent Sovereign, show mercy to us.

(2) The Envoy of [the Father (?)] heals souls.
gives joy [to all], and removes sorrows (?).

(4) [Lofty and] limitless, where Darkness never comes ...

(6) [All] the monasteries [are magnificent, and] the ... dwelling
[places.
For they are happy [in] the Light and know no pain.

(7) All who enter there, stay for eternity.
[Neither] blows not torture [ever] overcome them.

(18) [The clothes which they wear none] has made by hand.
[They are ever clean and bright, and] no ants (?) are in
[them.

(22) Their verdant garlands never fade,
and they are wreathed brightly, in numberless colors.

(23) Heaviness and drooping do not exist in their bodies,
and paralysis does not affect any of (their) limbs.

(24) Heavy sleep never overtakes their souls,
and deceptive dreams and delusions [are unknown among
[them].

(28) Hunger and anguish (are) not [known in that land].
(There is) no thirst, for ...

(29) [The waters] of all (its) lakes give out a wondrous
fragrance. [Floods and] frowning are never [known among
[them].

(32) Their walk is quicker by far than lightning.
In the bodies they possess, there is no sickness.

(33) The ... activities of all (Dark) Powers
... are not in them, nor attacks and conflicts.

(34) Fear and terror do not exist in those places,
and ... in those lands there is no destruction.

(35) ... the trees (?) do not shake down
... all the fruits.

(36) ... decay (?) [does not exist in] their fruit.
[Within and] without [it is all full of brightness].

(38) [All the gardens] give out fragrance, so that (?)...
[Bricks and thorns are] never [found] among [them].

(48) [Each who] ascends up to their land, and [who has the
[knowledge,
will praise] His manifestation, lauded and beneficent.

(49) None who is among ... has [a dark shadow].
[All the bodies] and appearances upon that land (are)
[radiant].

(51) Precious are they, [with forms that are free from injury]·
And feebleness and [age do not affect their limbs].

(59) They are joyous, (uttering) wonderful praises.
They [continually] do reverence to the Exalted and
[Bene[ficent] one.

(60) [All is filled] with happiness and sweet delightful song
... all the monasteries.

(64) The monasteries are all splendid, and fear is unknown
[therein ...

(66) Barking of dogs, calls of birds, confusing and troublesome
evil howling — they are not heard in (that) land.

(67) From any darkness and fog ... there is nothing within
the pure abodes.

(68) Full of Light is the(ir) Living Self; ever in gladness
and purity loving each other they are very beautiful.

(70) No Living Self dies among them...

[66, 67, 68 and 70: T.M. 278, Uighur translation: W.B. Henning, "A
Fragment of the Manichaean Hymn-Cycles in Old Turkish," *AM* n. s. 7
(1959): 123-24; Peter Zieme, *CAJ* 14 (1970): 233]

VI a

(1) Who will release me from all the pits and prisons,
    in which are gathered (?) lusts that are not pleasing?

(2) Who will take me over the flood of the tossing sea —
    the zone of conflict in which there is no rest?

(3) Who will save me from the jaws of all the beasts
    who destroy and terrify (?) one another without pity?

(4) Who will lead me beyond the walls and take me over the
                                                    [moats,
    which (are) full of fear and trembling from ravaging
                                                    [demons?

(5) Who will lead me beyond rebirths, and free me from
                                                [(them) all —
    and from all the waves, in which there is no rest?

(6) I weep for (my) soul, saying: May I be saved from this,
    and from the terror of the beasts who devour one another!

(7) The bodies of men, and of birds of the air,
    of fish of the sea, and four-footed creatures and of all
                                                    [insects —

(8) who will take me beyond these and save me from (them)
                                                    [all,
    so that I shall not turn and fall into the perdition of those
                                                    [hells

(9) so that I shall not pass through defilement in them, nor
                                            [return in rebirth,
    wherein all the kinds of plants (are) taken out in ...?

(10) Who will save me from the swallowing height (and?)
    the devouring deeps, which are all hell and distress?

IV b

(1) These will collapse upon the whole structure,
    and all the (Dark) Powers will perish in agony and
                                                    [perdition.

(2) And wretchedness will overtake all (its) inhabitants
and perdition of hell in which there is no mercy.

(3) Who will save me from these and take me beyond them all,
so that I shall not be devoured in the distress of those hell-
[deeps?

V

(1) Or who will save me from the pit of destruction,
and from the dark valley where all is harshness?

(2) — where all is anguish and the stab of death.
And helper and friend is there none therein.

(3) Never to eternity is there safety there.
(It is) all full of darkness and fume-filled fog.

(4) (It is) all full of wrath and there is no pity (?) there.
All who enter are pierced by wounds.

(5) (It is) waterless through drought, and hardened by hot
[winds.
No golden drop (of water) is ever (found) therein.

(6) Who will save me from this, and from all stabs,
and take me afar from all distress of hell?

(9) They are struck by merciless blows in the deep.
There is no health for all (their) sicknesses.

(10) Not all the lusts and the comfort of wealth
will help them in that hellish place.

(12) Not all (their) idols, altars and images
can save them from that hell.

(15) They shall [not] find [there] a pious (?) messenger,
[who] shall come [for them and] open [the gate of Hell].

(19) Who will take me far from [it, that] I may not plunge (?)
[into] them;
and that I may tumble and fall down into every bitter hell.

V c

(1) Their fragrant garlands are sacred and immortal;
their bodies are full of living pure drops.

(2) All with one mind praise one another; they bless (one
[another)
with living blessings, and become blessed for evermore.

(3) In my mind I remembered; and I wept [aloud] in [misery]
[(saying):
Who [will save] me from every terror and fear?

(4) Who will take me up to that happy realm,
so that joy shall be mine in union with all (its) inhabitants?

VI

(1) And while I thus wept and shed tears upon the ground,
I heard the voice of the Beneficent King.

VI a

(3) I shall save you from every ...
of the rebellious Powers who have frightened [you] with
[fear.

(4) [I shall release you] from all deceit and turbulence ...
[and] the torment of death.

(8) [I will make an end?] of the activity of all (forces of)
[destruction,
and all sickness which has dismayed you with death.

VI b

(22) I shall [free] you from the hands of the guardians of hell,
[who show no] mercy [to] spirit and soul.

VI c

(1) I shall take (you) eagerly and soar up upon wings,
high over all the (Dark) Powers and rebellious princes.

(2) I shall lead (you) into the primeval calm of that land
[(i.e., the New Paradise);
and I shall show (you) the Fathers, my (?) own divine
[entity (?).

(3) You shall rejoice in gladness, in blissful praises,
and you shall be without grief and ... forgetful of wretched-
[ness.

(4) You shall put on a radiant garment, and gird on Light;
and I shall set on your head the diadem of sovereignty.

(10) By a spiritual invocation [there was built?] on that
[structure?] the fortress,
high and vast, of the noble Em[peror].

(11) A palace is the dominion of the primeval First-born
[(i.e., the First Man),
for in it he clothes himself in gladness and binds on the
[diadem of sovereignty.

(12) And all (his) friends — he binds the diadem upon them,
and clothes their bodies in the garment of gladness.

(13) And all the believers and the pious Elect
he clothes in praise, and binds on them the diadem.

(14) They reign (now) in gladness, even as (once they had)
[been fettered for (their mere) name,
and (had) undergone anguish at the hands of (their) foes.

(20) [The return from] the ... Depth was obtained out of the
[Victory;
[for] the enemies are subdued, and the Height (lies) in
[front!

(21) ... [is] the day when He will reveal his form,
[the] beneficent [Father], the Lord of the Aeons of Light.

(22) [He will show that radiant shape] and brilliant, glorious
[form
[to all the Gods] who shall dwell there.

VII

(9) For through that will go out the chosen and all the benef-
[icent,
and all who knew the mystery and understood the belief.

(10) The Saviour of my soul revealed these things to me
... mighty ... through this ... greatness.

(11) [Upon that day of] departing he came with mercy to me,
[and saved me] from every anguish and prison.

(20) Truly you shall pass their border, and shall not be held
[at (their) watch-posts.
And you shall be saved from anguish ...

(22) [You shall lie] no longer within the foul body ...;
[you shall no more endure] that [heaviness] amid all
[sickness.

VIII

(1) [He] said unto me: What loathliness you have endured (?)
[in his company.
For that you shall receive the praise and the diadem of
[felicity.

(2) I shall take you up and show (you) (your) own origin.
And you shall rejoice in that place, and [dwell] in gladness
[evermore].

(11) [He] promised to me eternal completion
and the recompense for my devout torture.

(12) And even as I (had) strictly (?) believed and been patient
[in righteousness,
[so he gave] me the Victory above all the (Dark) Powers.

VIII a

(1) But you shall pass in safety by every ...
You shall reign in gladness and in freedom for evermore.

(2) You shall enter into that land ...
and shall rejoice in the gladness of that ...

(3) You shall abide in tranquillity ...
    and anguish [shall never overtake you] more.

Angad Rōshnān

I

(1) Rich Friend of the beings of Light! In mercy
    grant me [strength and] succour me with every gift!

(2) Array [my soul], O Lord! respond to me!
    [Succour me] in the midst of the foe!

(3) Make pass from me all the ravages
    of their deceitful body, that tortures me with pain.

(4) You are the friend, praised and beneficent!
    Free me from ...

(11) My soul weeps within,
    and cries out [at each] distress and stab.

(12) And the hour of life, and this carrion-form
    is ended for me, with (its) turbulent days.

(13) It was tossed and troubled as a sea with waves.
    Pain was heaped on pain, whereby they ravage my soul.

(14) On all sides the anguish reached (me);
    fire was kindled, and the fog (was full) of smoke.

(15) The wellsprings of Darkness had all been opened.
    The [giant] fishes transfixed me with fear.

(16) My soul was dismayed at the sight of their forms,
    for (they) became apparent in their dreadfulness;

(17) for all were hideous and dreadful to [behold].
    And the human form is not found among their bodies.

(18) All the demons, the banished Princes,
    transfixed me with fear, and dismayed me with anguish.

(19) Their fury gathered, like a sea of fire.
    The seething waves rose up that they might engulf me.

(22) For in every region gathered stormy winds (?)
and rain and the fume of all fogs,

(23) lightning and thunder and banked clouds (?) of hail,
the crash and roar of all the waves of the sea.

(24) The skiff rises up, lifted on the crest of the wave,
and glides down into the trough, to be hidden within.

(26) All the clamps become loosened by ...
The iron rivets are plucked out by ...

(27) Each yard [is dipped (?)] by these drownings.
And the masts are flung together (?) in the turmoil.

(28) The rudders (?) had dropped off into the sea.
[Fear grips] those on board.

(29) The helmsmen and all the pilots
weep bitterly and lament aloud.

I a

(1) Through continual redemptions
every hand, link, and shutter (?) of the prison becomes
[weakened (?)

(2) All the comets (?) quivered, and the stars were whirled
[about,
and each of the planets turned awry its course.

(3) The earth shook, my foundation beneath,
and the height of the heavens sank down above.

(4) All the rivers, the veins of my body,
dried up at (their) source (?) in every way.

(7) All my limbs have connection no longer.
When again they were broken, they reflected on existence.

(8) The reckoning of my days and months is ended.
Harm befell the course of the zodiac's wheel.

(11) The seal of my feet and the joints of my toes —
each link of the life of my soul was loosed.

(12) Each joint of my hands and of my fingers —
each was loosed and its seal taken off.

(13) All the gristly parts — their life (?) grew feeble.
And cold became each one of my limbs.

(14) My knees were fettered through fear,
and strength was drawn out of each leg.

I b

(12) And [when I saw] the Dark, the strength of my limbs
[collapsed;
and my soul moaned at all (its) forms.

III a

(1) Who shall save me ...
and make for me a path ...?

(2) Who shall make straight for me ...
by that path...?

III b

(12) Who shall free me from every ...
(from) blazing fire and the distress of [destruction]?

III c

(13) Who shall take off from me this ... body,
and clothe [me] in a new body...?

VI

(1) When I had said these words, with soul a-tremble,
I beheld the Saviour as he shone before me.

(2) I beheld the sight of all the Helmsmen,
who had descended with him to array my soul.

(3) I lifted up my eyes toward that direction,
and saw all deaths were hidden by the Envoy.

(4) All ravages had become remote from me,
and grievous sickness, and the anguish of their distress.

(5) The sight of them was hidden, their darkness had fled
[away.
And all (was divine) nature, without peer.

(6) [There shone forth] Light, elating and lovely
[and full] of gladness, pervading all my mind.

(7) In joy unbounded he spoke with me,
raising up my soul from deep affliction (?).

(8) To me he says, Come, spirit! fear not.
I am your Mind, your glad tidings of hope.

(9) And you are the ... garment of my body,
which brought dismay to the Powers (of Darkness) ...

(10) I am your Light, radiant, primeval,
your Great Mind and complete hope.

(21) You are my word, and my panoply of war,
[which saved me] fully [from the fight], and [from] all
[sinners.

(32) From each dungeon (?) shall I release you,
bearing you afar from all wounds [and afflictions].

(33) I shall lead (you) forth from this torture (?) ...
You shall no [more] feel fear at each encounter.

(42) Beloved! beauty of my bright nature!
From these shall I lead you forth, and [from] all prisons.

(43) I shall save you from all perdition,
and free you for ever [from] all wounds.

(44) And all the filth and corrosion that you have passed
[through,
[I shall cleanse] from you through perfect Light.

(45) And the deep of the sea wherein you have gone through
[these drownings,
I shall deliver (you) from that and from all the waves.

(49) I shall set you free from every sickness,
and from every distress at which you have wept.

(50) I shall not wish to leave you longer in the hands of the
[Sinner;
for you are my own, in truth, for ever.

(51) You are the buried treasure, the chief of my wealth,
and the pearl which (is) the beauty of all the Gods.

(52) And I am the righteousness sown in your limbs,
and (in) the stature of (your) soul — the gladness of
[your Mind.

(53) And you are my beloved, the Love in my limbs;
and the heroic Mind, the essence of my limbs.

(54) And I am the Light of your whole structure,
your soul above and base of life.

(55) And from the holiness of my limbs did you descend in
[the beginning
into the dark places, and did become their Light.

(56) And from you a diadem was bound on all (our) foes.
And it became apparent and held sway during the hours
[of tyranny.

(57) And for your sake was there battle and tremor
in all the heavens and the bridges of the earths.

(58) And for your sake ran [and sped]
all the (Dark) Powers over ...

(59) And for your sake were bound [the Princes]
and all the (Dark) Powers, and ...

(61) For your sake shone forth the Apostles and became appa-
[rent,
who reveal the Light above, and uncover the root of
[Darkness.

(62) And for your sake the Gods went forth and became ap-
[parent,
and they struck down Death, and Darkness they slew.

(63) And you are the exalted Trophy
and the sign of Light that puts Darkness to flight.

(64) And I am come forth to save (you) from the Sinner,
to make (you) whole from pain, and to bring gladness to
[your heart.

(65) And all you have desired of me I shall bestow upon you,
and I shall make new your place within the lofty kingdom.

(66) And I shall open before you the gates in all the heavens,
and shall make smooth your path, free from terror and
[vexation.

(67) And I shall take (you) with might, and enfold (you) with
[love,
and lead (you) to (your) home, the blessed abode.

(68) And for ever shall I show to you the noble Father (i.e.,
[the First Man);
and I shall lead you in, into (his) presence, in pure
[raiment.

(69) And I shall show to you the Mother of the beings of Light.
And for ever shall you rejoice in lauded happiness.

(70) And I shall reveal to you the holy Brethren,
the noble (?) ..., who are filled with happiness.

(71) And for ever shall you [dwell] joyful among them all,
beside all the Jewels and the venerable Gods.

(72) And fear and death shall never overtake (you more),
nor ravage, distress and wretchedness.

(73) And rest shall be yours in the place of salvation,
in the company of all the Gods and those who dwell in
[quietness.

VII

(1) Come, spirit, fear no more!
Death has fallen, and sickness fled away.

(2) And the term of troubled days is ended,
and its terror departed amid clouds of fire.

(3) Come, spirit, step forth!
Let there be no desire for the house of affliction,

(4) which is wholly destruction and the anguish of death.
Truly you were cast out from your native abode.

(5) And all the pangs you have suffered in hell
you have undergone for this, in the outset and beginning.

(6) Come yet nearer, in gladness without regret;
and lie not content in the dwelling of death.

(7) Turn not back, nor regard the shapes of the bodies,
which lie (there) in wretchedness, they and (their) fellows.

(8) And see, they return through every rebirth,
and through every agony and every choking (?) prison.

(9) And see, they are reborn among all (kinds of) creatures,
and their voice is heard in burning sighs.

(10) Come yet nearer, and be not fond of
this beauty that perishes in all (its) varieties.

(11) And it falls and melts as snow in sunshine.
And there is no abiding for any fair form.

(12) And it withers and fades as a broken rose,
that wilts in the sun, whose grace is destroyed.

(13) Yet come, you spirit, and be not fond
of the sum of hours and the fleeting days.

(14) And turn not back for every outward show.
Desire (is) death, and leads to destruction.

(15) Hence, spirit, come!...
I shall lead (you) to the height, [to your native abode].

(17) Remember, O spirit! look on the anguish (?)
that (you have) borne through the fury of all (your)
[ravagers.

(18) And regard the world and the prison of creation;
for all desires will be swiftly destroyed.

(19) Terror, fire and ruin will overtake
all those who dwell therein.

(20) The height will be shattered with all (its) dwellings;
all the heavens will fall down into the deep.

(21) And the trap of destruction will swiftly close
upon those deceivers who brag therein.

(22) And the whole dominion, with the brilliance of all the
stars — ruin will come upon them, and the pang of their
indignity.

(23) All the Princes and the border-rebels (will suffer)
for ever in wretchedness within the blazing fire.

(25) The whole of life, from every seed and [stem],
will swiftly be wrecked and brought to perdition.

(35) The parts of the dead souls will be [fettered]
in the tomb of death where all is blackness,

(36) and (where) all (is) malediction of Darkness ...;
truly they will be clad in the distress of ...

VII a

(1) And they will become the bricks (?) (which are) spoilt
[and smashed,
which are not fit to go up to the keepers of the Building.

(2) They will fall into the deep and be devoured in death.
They will clothe themselves in darkness, distress, and fire.

(3) And they will nevermore find one to pity them.
And none will open for them the gate of hell.

(4) And they will be seared with sorrow amid all the quakings.
They will groan and shriek at (their) bondage for ever.

(5) And there is none who will hear (?) and have mercy upon
[them,
for the sake of ... destruction.

(11) Be glad of heart on this day of departing,
[for] sickness is ended, and all your rigours.

(12) And you shall go forth out of this deceiver (i.e., the body),
which has made you faint through distress and the agony
[of death.

(13) You were held back within the abyss, where all is turmoil;
and you were made captive (?) in every place.

(14) You were suspended amid all rebirths.
And you have suffered ravage amid all cities.

VIII

(2) My soul is saved from all the sins
which day by day [oppressed] (me) [ever] in anguish.

(3) And the dark, hot (?) distress is taken from me
which at the outset, in the beginning, made me captive in...

(4) I am clothed with a garment of Light...
Every kind of ... is taken off from me.

(5) And I am passed beyond the pain and anguish of their
[bodies.
Every ... has become remote from [me].

(6) And I am arrayed and succored by the Saviour of my
[spirit,
through the ... power, which never was constricted.

(11) Those who are homomorphic with the demons will pass
again through all the prisons and the cycle of death.

(12) And I saw that it (i.e., the abandoned body) became dark,
[and there is no light therein;
hideous in appearance and overpowering in form.

(13) The Saviour said to me: Spirit! behold the husk
(you have) abandoned in the deep in terror [and] destruc-
[tion.

(14) Truly for you it was a deceptive partner,
a distressful prison in every hell.

(15) And truly for you it was an unruly death.
which [severed] your soul from life for ever.

(16) And truly for you it was a path of stumbling
     which was wholly deeds of dread, and much sickness.

[Mary Boyce, *The Manichaean Hymn-Cycles in Parthian*, London Oriental Series, no. 3. (Oxford, 1954,) p. 66 ff.; cf. Mary Boyce, "Some remarks on the present state of the Iranian Manichaean MSS. from Turfan, together with additions and corrections to 'Manichaean Hymn-Cycles in Parthian'," *MIO*, vol. 4, no. 2, Berlin, 1956, p. 320 ff.]

X. Jesus in Manichaeism

It is generally assumed that for Mani the historical Jesus had no importance, but only the transcendent Jesus. This, however, is not quite accurate, since the physical framework around the historical Jesus was of exceedingly great significance for Mani. The physical life-history of Christ was in fact pedagogically ideal for rendering intelligible the magnificent symbolism that was to express the difficult environment of the portions of light in the prison of matter. Mani both knew and employed the gospels of the New Testament, and himself appears to have been influenced by the language of the parables: [45]

(a) ... they are. That wheat (i.e., the Living Self)
    he collects. And
    he carries (it) to his grain vessel
    from which it went out. And
    he himself also goes into his
    house, from which
    he came, for that reason that
    he has performed the thing for
    the sake of which he came and (because) he has mowed
    and collected that for
    the sake of which he came, and because that
    [wh]eat has been collected in his grain vessel
    . . . .

(6) '... we will receive and under protection guide him
    on the straight paths.'
    And this
    testimony that he
    spoke is truth.
    Further he said: "See
    that no one leads you
    astray, for in my name
    many will come
    and speak thus:
    'We belong to Jesus,

and his time has come.'
And many they will lead astray."

[M 6005, Middle Persian: Ed. W. Sundermann, lines 2062-2089; *Cat.* p. 118]

In (a) we, no doubt, have a parable about the Living Self, its being lost and regained by the First Man (the farmer). The quotation from Luke 21,8 closely corresponds to the Arabic version of Tatian's *Diatessaron*.

Another text is M 500 c, given here not because it is very illuminating as far as content is concerned, being, unfortunately, too fragmentary, but because it is another testimony to the popularity and pedagogical usefulness of the parables of Jesus (cf. Matthew 13, Mark 4 and Luke 8). It is, however, presented in an entirely Manichaean interpretation, with Mani as the sower choosing the good soil (the Hearers) for the seed of the Church:

Now ...
... what was sown
[... pre]pared ...
... brings forth, is the [*N*]*ous*.
[What] grew [on stony pla]ces [becomes no] gain.
[the ot]her that grew in the desert
[... bri]ngs forth ... is the Evil Thought,
[and its] fruit is harshness.

[M 500 c, Parthian: Ed. W. Sundermann, lines 1838-1845; *Cat.* p. 34]

The parable about the hard conditions of the soul (the boy) in the body (the prison with the three doors) and in a world ruled by Evil (the king and his daughter desiring it) and its hope of salvation through the Saviour (here the bull that may be Vahman or Jesus or any giver of redeeming knowledge) is, in its exposition, methodically very close to New Testament passages, e.g. Matthew 13, 37 ff.; Mark 4, 14; Luke 8, 11 ff.:

"When you take that boy here,
g[ive] me as a wife (to him)." The king
three times sent off horses and men,
saying: "Go and bring the boy."
They went off and round
the tree they sto[od].

They spoke: "The king calls (you)."
[The bo]y ... not ... . Three
times the men ...
he did ... (and) killed. The king
said: "What am I to do now?
The horses and the men are annihilated,
(my) daughter is dying." Then
there was an old woman. She said: "Another
... ." The king said:
"How will you bring (him)?" Then she ...
took wine and a lamb,
went off (and) [sa]t down under the tree. The lamb
she bound, (and) she killed (it) at [the tail].
The boy said: "Kill at the neck!"
She killed (it) at the tail. Then
she said to the boy: "Come,
show it to me! " Then the
boy came down from the tree,
(thinking): "I will show it to her." The woman gave (him) wine.
As soon as he had drunk this drink,
he became unconscious. Then on
an ass she piled (him) up. To the king she to[ok] (him).
He gave (him) to the girl. In [the palace?]
he made three doors. And two of them (were)
of copper (and) of tin. [For] the
inner (door) he put iron without number
(and) tin without number together (and)
made a door thereof. When the boy
came to consciousness, he played his flute. The bull
heard (it), it came, two doors
it broke down, and to
the third door it came, with power
they were broken down, and
one of its horns was broken. It went off.
robbed and abducted the boy.
To the boy it said: "According to ..."
.   .   .   .
... all ...

The sovereign is Ahrmēn.
... the old woman
... the three flutes
are [the five comma]ndments for the Elect.
The three doors are the fire, the lust
[and the greed ...]

[M 46 and M 652 R, Middle Persian: Ed. W. Sundermann, lines 1634-
1683; *Cat.* p. 5 and 45]

The Passion was a particular favorite (the sufferings of the
Light!):

The Jews in ... gone out from the land ... Thus he (or: it)
showed that in the morning the teachers, the priests, the scribes
and the leaders of the community deliberated and, one with the
other, took counsel to kill him. And they sought false witnesses
but their testimony, one with the other, did not agree. And they
brought forth two others, and they said: "This man says: I am
able to destroy this temple that is made with hands, and within
three days build (another) that is made without hands'."
And (not) even so (did their) testimony (agree) with ... Truly
(?) ... Hereafter shall you see the Son of Man, when he is sitting
on the right hand of the Power, (and) when he is coming in
(the clouds) of heaven. Then the High Priest (rent his) clothes and
said: "To me (?) ...." And they said to each other: "... what
the witness has said (?), now all of us further ... of his mouth
we have heard (it) ... ." ... one must kill ... Pilate ...

May you (plur.) save (us) from this that has come over him,
when — may all of us know (it) — when also Jesus Christ,
the Lord of all of us, was crucified — so it (the text)? shows
about him —: They seized him like a sinner and dressed him
in a scarlet coat and gave him a cane in his right hand, and they
pay reverence ... mocking him (?) (and) they say: "Long live
our Messiah," and they took him to the cross... ."

[M 4570, Parthian: W. Sundermann, "Christliche Evangelientexte in der
Überlieferung der iranisch-manichäischen Literatur," *MIO* 14 (1968):
390 ff.; *Cat.* p. 100; the text is a rather free rendering of Tatian's *Diatessaron*
with quotations from Matthew 26 and 27, Mark 14, and Luke 22]

... Jesus ... when he went (?) into ... the governor, and Pilate ...
asked: "Are you really king in the House of Jacob and the

Tribe of Israel?" the just Interpreter (i.e., Jesus) answered
Pilate: "My kingdom is not of this world." Then under pres-
sure of the Jews, (he was) bound ... to Herod the King ... he
stood (there) silent, and Herod the King ... dressed (him) in
a garment ... put a crown of thorns on (his) head ... For prostra-
tion they come, cover his head, smite (him) with a cane on the
chin and the mouth, spit in his eye and say: "Our Lord Messiah,
the Provident One." But three times the Romans came, and
three times they fell down headlong. For always he, beautiful
of nature and voice, wanders (?) in the power of wonder ...
living ... ."

[M 132, partly combined with M 5861, Parthian: *HR* II, p. 36-37, W.
Sundermann, op. cit., p. 394 ff.; *Cat.* p. 11 and 116]

Characteristic of this Manichaean text is, as Sundermann
rightly points out, the marked tendency to free Pilate from guilt,
further stressed by the respectful attitude of the Roman soldiers.

"Lord ... you destroy ... ." Beautifully Jesus answered the Jews:
"Ask those who are (my) disciples now, what the teaching is
(like) that I have taught them, and the deeds that I have ordered
them. Caiaphas the High Priest together with all the Jews put
on malice and anger. And with torture causing deadly pain
they tortured Jesus the beloved one very much .... But humbly
to the Building of God Ohrmizd...

[From M 734, Parthian: W. Sundermann, op. cit., p. 397 f.; *Cat.* p. 49]

The Building of God Ohrmizd *(Ōhrmizd bag rāz)* here, no
doubt, is especially used about the New Paradise, the resting
place for the redeeming gods during their struggle to save the
bound Light, erected upon the New Building or the Great Building
that was built by the Great Builder at the command of the
Third Messenger (see p. 125).

He crucified (him) together with sinners. Then Pilate also
wrote a wonderful document in Greek and Latin *(yōnāv ud
frōmāv*(Roman)) and hung it on the cross. And he writes: "This
is Jesus of Nazareth, the King of the Jews. Whoever reads this,
may he know that sin was not found in him."

[M 4574, a "new" text, found by the late Prof. H.J.F. Junker, Parthian:
W. Sundermann, op. cit., p. 400 f.]

Particularly interesting is the Parthian text M 18, [46] one of the crucifixion hymns, in that it appears in part to have had the apocryphal Gospel of Peter as a basis: " '... (in) truth he is the Son of God,' and Pilate answered: 'See, I have no part in the blood of this Son of God.' In the following lines of the fragment there are, however, several divergences so that the idea immediately suggests itself that a Harmony of the Gospels, including the Gospel of Peter, has been used. Theodore bar Kōnai indeed says: "Although he (Mani) thought completely paganly, he also wished to use the name of Messiah." He was the apostle of Jesus (*frēstag 'ig Yišō*). Jesus brought the same message as Mani and came from the same God. The enemies of Jesus were therefore Mani's enemies. This is made apparent with all the clarity that can be desired in the interesting—and, concerning the historical Jesus, quite unpolemic—Sogdian fragment TM 393, where Judas Iscariot is condemned for having slandered Jesus and Satan (s't't'nh, fem.!) as having corrupted the Christian church. [47]

Only the fundamental Christian dogma of the suffering and death of the Son of God could Mani not accept. His concept of Jesus is purely docetic. The divine could not suffer, could not participate in evil.

> Grasp, all believers, the truth of Christ,
> learn and wholly understand His secret:
> He changed His form and appearance
>
> [M 24 R 4-8 = M 812 V 1-4, Parthian: W.B. Henning, "Bráhman," *TPS*, 1944, p. 112; *Cat.* p. 3 and 55]

The divine could not manifest itself as a human body, it would be to identify Light with Matter, it would be blasphemy; indeed worse, it would destroy any possibility of salvation. Therefore, "the sons of God" from *Gen.* 6.2. are in Mani's *Book of the Giants* denied their divine origin and transformed into demons, *dēvān*. [48]

It was important for Mani to give his audience an image of Jesus as concrete and as unambiguous as possible. In *Shābuhragān*, dedicated to the Sasanid king Shāhpuhr I and the only one of Mani's own works written in Middle Persian, the great pericope on the Final Judgment from Matthew 25.31 ff. is retold. With an audacious although quite unpolemic interpolation into this text, handed down unfortunately only fragmentarily, he seeks to free his concept of Jesus from an interpretation, here particularly obvious, in the direction of the earthly-human:

... they will ... and say: "We are God's teachers. Go then according to the advice that we have given." And most people will be deceived, and they will behave (lit. go) according to their desire for evil-doing. And the righteous one who does not believe in his own religion, he also will be joined to them (i.e., the sinners). And at that time, when in the world things will be like that, then on earth and in the sky and in the sun and the moon and the signs of the zodiac and the stars, a great sign will appear.

Then God Khradēshahr (i.e., Jesus), he who in the beginning gave wisdom and knowledge to this male creature, the first man, the first mortal, and who also hereafter period after period and time after time sent wisdom and knowledge to men, he also in this end time, close to the (final) Restoration, (he), the very same Khradēshahr ...

then in ... he will stand; and a great call will be called out; and the whole world will be made aware. And these gods that in the universe of heavens and earths are Lord of the House, Lord of the Village, Lord of the Tribe and Lord of the Country, Lord of the Watch-post (i.e., the five sons of the Living Spirit), and oppressor (or: slanderer) of the demons, they will bless Khradēshahr and be sovereigns of the men that are in the world. And all the demons will come before him and pay homage and take his orders. And the man full of greed and evil-doing and lust (?) will be repentant. And thereafter God Khradēshahr will send angels to the east and to the west and they will go. And the righteous man with his friends and the evildoers together with those of the same doing will come together before Khradēshahr, and the righteous will say to him: " ... our Lord, if it is pleasing to you, ... we wish to say to you."

And God Khradēshahr will answer them thus: "See me and be glad. But he who has sinned against you I shall judge for you and call to account, but all you wish to say to me I know." He then blesses them and calms their hearts and places them at right side, and all the gods stand around in joy. And he separates the evildoers from the righteous and places them on his left side and condemns them; and he says thus to them: "He who

rises in a lie(?) will not shine (?), as whatever sin you have committed ... suffering ... you have committed against me."
... and to the righteous standing on his right side he says thus: "Peace be with you ... for I was hungry and thirsty, and you gave me all kinds of food; I was naked and you clothed me; I was sick, and you made me well; I was bound, and you released me; I was a prisoner, and you delivered me; I was an exile and a wanderer, and you took me into your house." Then the friends of the righteous will show deep reverence and say to him: "Lord, you are God and immortal, and greed and lust have no power over you. You are not hungry and thirsty, and pain and torment comes not to you. When was it we did you this service?" And Khradēshahr answers them thus: "What you have done ..., that you have done ... towards me. And I shall give you Paradise as a reward ... ." ... and he will give them great joy.

Then says he thus to the evildoers standing on his left side: "You evildoers, worldly ones, guided by greed, evil and ... have you been. I complain of you, for I was hungry and thirsty, and you gave me no food whatsoever; I was naked and you did not clothe me; I was sick and you did not make me well. I was a prisoner and an exile, and you did not take me into your house." And the evildoers will say thus unto him: "Our God and Lord! When was it that you were so distressed and we did not save you?" And Khradēshahr says to them: "What you had in mind against the righteous, you have sinned against me. This is why I was complaining of you. And sinners you are, since you were the grief (?) and the enemies of the righteous. And you caused affliction and showed no mercy. Against ... are you guilty in sin ... ." Then he places angels over these evildoers, and they will take them up and cast them into hell ... and when God Khradēshahr will be in the world, then day, month and year will stop. And harm will overcome greed and lust and pain and torment ... and evil years and disgrace they will shake off, and they will sin no more. And wind, water and fire will flow through the world, and the rain ... will fall ... Tombs and sepulchres they shall pass, and they (i.e., the survivors of the Great War that had just taken place) shall see them, and their relatives are ..., ... they will say : "Woe unto them that died and went out (of the world) in the evil time (i.e., before the happiness of Restoration); but who would lift their heads up from their resting-place and let them see this joy in which we live now?"

[M 473, M 475, M 477, M 482 R, Middle Persian: A. Ghilain, "Un feuillet manichéen reconstitué," *Le Muséon* 59 (1946); 539 f., *HR* II: 11 ff., W.B. Henning, "A Farewell to the Khagan of the Aq-Aqatärān," *BSOAS* 14 (1952): 516-17; *Cat.* p. 31-32]

... he wanted to break the fire-waves in order to boil everything in the fire. The noble Sovereign (i.e., Jesus) changed his garment and appeared in might before Satan: Then earth and heaven quaked, and Sammail (i.e., Satan; a name also used by the dualistic Bulgarian Bogomils) fell into the abyss. The true Interpreter (i.e., Jesus) had mercy on the Light that the enemies had devoured. From the deep pool of destruction he led it up to that place of activity from which it had descended.

Reverence to you, Son of Greatness (i.e., Jesus), who set your righteous ones free; now also protect the teacher Mar Zakō, the great shepherd of your bright flock, Wake up, brothers, Elect: On this day (came) the salvation of the souls, in the month of Mihr on the fourteenth, when Jesus, the Son of God, went into Parinirvana. Give attention, all believers in God: When the time of accomplishment came, the demons of wrath came to know about the Son of Man. And the lord of that doctrine of sin ... put on trick, (and) they taught the same (?). The twelve thrones (i.e., heaven) above were agitated; poison was poured upon the creation below, upon the sons; and the cup of death was prepared. The Jews, the "servants of the Highest God," slily made harm (?); the slanderer fell; in his place (?) they battle with the Son of Man. They plan what is sinful; with deceit they bring in false witnesses. The unfortunate Satan himself, who always troubled the apostles, disturbed the flock of the Messiah. He made the traitor (?) Iscariot his mount ... . He (Iscariot) with a hand-kiss (?) pointed him out (to the nightwatch), gave him over to his enemies, renounced the Son of God ... (and) sacrificed his own lord and teacher for the bribe that the Jews gave (him).

[M 104, Parthian: *MM* III, p. 881-883, *JRAS* 1944, p. 143, note 6; *Cat.* p. 9]

A clear and undisguised attack on the dogma of the divinity of the Son of Man is contained in the small and unfortunately badly-preserved text M 28, which turns polemically against

Christian and Zarathustrian (see p. 14). The Christians are condemned because, in their delusion, they invoke Maryam's son *(bar
Maryam)* as the Son of God *(pus i Adōnai)*. It was Maryam's son
who suffered and died, not the son of the living God. Maryam's
son could not be the Son of God, since a god does not feel himself
betrayed and deserted; a god is not crucified by the Father. If
Jesus of the Christians claims to have conquered death, it is strange
and inconsequent that, in his misery, he called to the Father:
"Why have you crucified me? "*(kū-t čim kird hēm ubdār).*[49] Such an
exclamation excludes divinity!

But as Jesus the Splendor he is one of the most popular figures
in Manichaean theology. He is the redeemer *par excellence*. Even
where religion became degenerate and magic gained ground, he
retained his popularity as the one people called upon in prayer
for help in all vicissitudes of life:

> Protect me in my corporeal existence, Jesus,
> oh Lord, save my soul
> from this birth-death (i.e., *samsāra*, the cycle of rebirths);
> save my soul from this
> birth-death ...
> Full of love is your throne, bright ...
>
> [M 311, last part, Parthian :*HR* II: p. 67; *Cat.* p. 22]

Hymns to Jesus

> ... all in one mind.
> And we will stretch out our hand in prayer
> and direct our eye towards this figure of yours.
> And we will open our mouth to invoke you
> and prepare our tongue for praise.
> You we invoke, you who are Life entire,
> and you we praise, Jesus the Splendor, New Aeon.
> You are, you are the Righteous [God],
> the [noble] Healer, the most beloved Son, the most loved Self (?).
> Come in peace, liberated Sovereign!
> Come for aid, good Spirit, Apostle for peace!
> Helper of the meek and Conqueror of the aggressors!
> Come in peace, new Sovereign!

Come in peace, Redeemer of the captives and Healer of the
[wounded!
Come in peace, Awakener of the sleeping and Arouser of the
[sleepy!
You who make the dead arise!
Come in peace, mighty God and holy Voice!
Come in peace, true Word, great Brilliance and abundant
[Light!
Come in peace, new Sovereign and new Day!
Come in peace, Beginning of the Worlds and Life of the many!
Come in peace, Gift of the good, Blessing of the meek and
[Adoration of the holy!
Come in peace, loving Father and beneficent Judge of those
who have taken refuge with you!
Come in peace, Father, you who are our powerful protection
[and firm confidence!
Come in peace, [Destroyer of (?)] the aggressors

.   .   .   .

Now ... Beneficent One, [peace (?)] be upon us!
And have mercy upon us and love us, Benefactor, (you) who
[(are) all love!
And do not reckon us together with the disturbers!
Take care of those who took refuge, and have mercy upon us!
Oh most beloved and loving!
We have seen you, New Aeon, and we have fallen at your
[feet, (you) who (are) all love!
And full of joy we have seen you, loving Lord!
And your name we profess, M and S (i.e., Messiah).
Separate us from amid the sinful,
and free us from amid the aggressors!
Oh Lord, we are your own, have mercy upon us!
Come quickly and in haste and conquer the sinners!
For they have become proud and have spoken thus:
"We are the ones! And there are none like us!"
Oh, be powerful and cast the aggressors ... and the impostors
[(i.e., a kind of demon) down!
The ungrateful one (?) who ...
[We praise your] name that (is) all brilliance,

and the noble greatness of all (your) heritage.
Praise be to this your name, Father!
And honor to your Greatness!
So be it still and for ever and ever!

[M 28 II, Middle Persian: *MM* II: 312:16; *Cat.* p. 4 .See A. Périkhanian, "Notes sur le lexique iranien et arménien," *RÉA* (1968): 16 ('z'dyh)]

The spread of Christianity eastwards into the heart of Asia made possible an extensive use of the name of Jesus. From the Atlantic to China, Manichaean missionaries could with equanimity include Jesus in their sermons without being misunderstood. It is therefore not surprising that hymns to Jesus were written one after another.

For Jesus was the doctor (*bēšaz*, cf. "Jesus, the good doctor" *(āsyā ṭābā)*, the Syriac *Doctrina Addai* f. 3 a, line 7, ed. G. Phillips, 1879) who could give health to sick mankind, light for the world's progress, the realm of light itself, in brief, *Gnosis*. Indeed, his popularity might even lead to a dangerous proximity to pure heresy. This appears from the question which the disciples asked the teacher, why Jesus (ay tängri) preceded the Father of Greatness (äzrua tängri) himself (von le Coq, "Türkische Manichaica III," *APAW* 1922, p. 12). "I petition only that Jesus will have mercy and liberate me from the bondage of all devils and spirits. Bestow the medicine of the great Law and let me be healed." So it reads in the extensive hymn cycle *Mo Ni Chiao Hsia Pu Tsan,*[50] which is part of the great body of translated Manichaean literature in Chinese.

The hymns usually include no detailed theology of Jesus. For this purpose, religious poetry is of course not generally the best means. But they are a moving expression of the confidence felt for the redeemer Jesus and his mighty powers. Although it would be tempting to consider the Jesus hymns as stagnant sacred poetry of no originality, it is probably nearer the truth to interpret every word as having meaning, being intended as a link in a greater context where man's sincerest hopes surge forward and become a cry for redemption.

A DIALOGUE BETWEEN JESUS THE SPLENDOR
AND HIS ALTER EGO, JESUS THE BOY, THE BOUND LIGHT.

[Jesus] . . . .

[For] from stupefaction the four worlds are agitated; and you, Friend, endure here for the sake of the souls so that through you salvation may come forth.

[Boy]   The honor and service shown me time after time by you, God, are obvious to all eyes. But only of this (time) I complain, when you ascended and left me behind like an orphan.

[Jesus] Remember, oh Boy, the head of the battle-stirrers, the Father God Ohrmizd who rose up from the darkness. Then

(also) he abandoned the sons in the depth for the sake of the great gain.

[Boy]   Hear my prayer, Commander with the dear name: If you do not set me free this time, send (then) many gods, so that I can gain the victory over those doing harm.

[Jesus] The Great Nous I gave instructions to send Envoys to you, when ... had come. (So) you, too, like the burdened Light ones, show your longanimity!

[Boy]   The world and its children were alarmed; for my sake Zarathustra came down to the realm of Persia, and he showed truth, selected my limbs from the Lights of the seven climes.

[Jesus] When Satan learned that he had come down, he sent out the demons of wrath. Earlier than the counter-attack, Beloved One, harm was over you because of their action and the perverted wisdom.

[Boy]   The complaint went off from me at the time when Shakya-muni Buddha ... me. He opened the door of salvation to the fortunate souls that he redeemed among the Indians.

[Jesus] Because of the arts and the wisdom that you received from Buddha, Dibat (i.e., the Babylonian name of the planet Venus), the great virgin, envied you. When he (i.e.,

Buddha) went into Nirvana, he told you: 'Await Mai-treya [51] here!' "

[Boy] Then Jesus showed pity for the second time, and he sent out the four pure winds [52] to help me, bound the three winds, [53] destroyed Jerusalem together with the mounts of the demons of wrath.

[Jesus] The cup of poison and death, hatred, was poured over you, Boy, by Iscariot together with the sons of Israel, and also much other anguish that came ...

[Boy] ... fettered ... of the apostles is small; and the two troops which attack me are numberless.

[Jesus] Your great battlefield (is) like that of God Ohrmizd and your collection of treasure like that of the Chariots of Light; also this Living Self which (is) in flesh and wood you can save from Greed (Āz).

[Boy] All three gods took care of this child; and they sent to me Mar Mani the savior, who delivered me from the servitude in which I served the enemies, against my will, in fear.

[Jesus] I gave you, my adjutant, freedom from ... .

[M 42, Parthian: *MM* III: 878-81; *Cat.* p. 5]

Jesus is referred to as the redeemer both in Middle Persian (South-west Iranian) and in Parthian (North-west Iranian) texts, often together with the Virgin of Light and Vahman; these three who form a unity so to say. They are "the three to come who bring our souls life."

All deities in the third act of the Manichaean drama of creation are gods of redemption. This at least can be established, however complicated the position and function of the individual deity may otherwise be. But, of these deities, Jesus appears more and more strongly as the god of redemption *par excellence*. For the Chinese Manichaeans, Jesus is "the Second Greatness" *(vazragīft)* imme-diately following the Father of Light, a position to which the Third Messenger was usually entitled. In North African Mani-chaeism also, the Third Messenger was completely replaced by Jesus. Augustine, for example, makes no reference whatever to the Third Messenger. Under these circumstances it was not surprising that Manichaean missionary preaching had so tremendous a success when it proclaimed Jesus as redeemer and giver of life, doctor and paraclete for a new and better existence where the power of darkness was finally broken. Such strains sounded singularly promising and also irresistibly compelling, all the more so since they came from missionaries who had a keen sense of what should be said and a deep psychological understanding of how to say it.

XI. The Manichaean Myth

When Mani and his disciples explained in writing and speech their large myth complex, details were set forth in abundance. Everything centered on the great aim of creating man's desire for redeeming knowledge. Mani and his missionaries knew the importance of repetition. When well-known material and names occurred again and again, a feeling of security and confidence was produced in the minds of the listeners. Already Homer understood that. But in the case of Mani the subject was theology, and exposition of vital knowledge. It was established with the strength of repetition through the fixed myth outline that was the foundation, but also through supplementing details that to all appearance has full *licentia poetica* or, in other words, neither could nor must be explained. Mani very likely did feel that one might be lured into conviction that every detail in the interpretations of the doctrine had a deeper sense or a wider range than permissible. His picture book, the *Ārdahang*, apparently had the intention of a clear and unambiguous settling of those elements of his teaching that really mattered.

According to the Manichaeans' general view of the world, there were in the beginning, when heaven and earth had not yet come into existence, two principles *(dō bun)*, Light, the good, and Darkness, the evil. They were of equal strength, but otherwise having nothing in common, separated by a boundary. In the world of Light the Father of Greatness (also named the Father of Light, the First Parent, God Zurvān, the Righteous God, the God of Paradise, Bonus Pater, Benignus Pater, the Good One (in Titus of Bostra), etc.) sits enthroned with the twelve Diadems of Light. He is surrounded by his twelve sons, first-born, the twelve Aeons, with the "Aeons of the Aeons," who are in *aër ingenitus*. The Father of Greatness himself is *pater ingenitus* and the Realm of Light is *terra ingenita*, the Everlasting Paradise. But ultimately these *tres res ingenitae* are one, the Father alone:

> Felix said: "Yes indeed there are three, the Unbegotten Father, the Unbegotten Land, and the Unbegotten Air." Augustine

said: "All that is one substance *(una substantia)*?" Felix said: "Yes". [*Contra Felicem Manichaeum* I, 18.]

Indeed, this is the Manichaean principle of identity in a state of pure cultivation! The *tres res ingenitae* furthermore are included in the "Five Greatnesses," together with the 12 sons and the Aeons of the Aeons. To judge from the descriptions of the Realm of Light, the problematic Uighur God of the Wind *(yil tängri)* [54] — *tängri*, god, divine, because everything in the Realm of Light is at the same time an "expression" of the Father of Greatness and the Father of Greatness himself — seems only to be one of the ingredients, probably completely or partly evoked by the idea of *aër ingenitus*, in a general, popularized description of paradise.

The Realm of Darkness, which has been constructed by negative analogy with the Realm of Light, is ruled by the Prince of Darkness Ahrmēn, who with his hosts desires the delightful things of the Realm of Light and means mischief. In order to forestall him the Father of Greatness evokes the Mother of the Living (the Mother of Life, the Mother-of-the-god-Ohrmizd), who then calls forth the First Man Ohrmizd. The joy at this "prince, son of a king" is great in the Realm of Light. With his five sons (the Five Elements, the Fivefold God) as armour, the First Man rushes into the fight in order to annihilate the Powers of Darkness; but the result is an (apparently) complete defeat. Light and Darkness become mixed. For Christian polemicists, this was synonymous with Satan's having the ability to conquer God, at least temporarily. The Syrian patriarch, Givargis I, in a letter written in the year 680, refers to it as the lunacy, madness *(shenāyūthā)* of the Manichaeans.

In the second act of the great drama everything is concentrated on the liberation of the First Man. The Father of Greatness therefore evokes the Friend of the Lights; the latter evokes the Great Builder (Bān rabbā, Bāmyazd), from whom the Living Spirit, Spiritus Vivens, the Demiurge (Mihryazd in Southwest Iranian texts), issues. The Living Spirit is the performing principle proper. With his five sons (the Holder of Glory or Splenditenens, the King of Honour or Rex honoris, Light Adamas, the Glorious King or Rex gloriosus, and the Bearer or Atlas), who constitute a parallel to the five sons of Ohrmizd, the Elements of Light, *amahrāspandān*, as his helpers he proceeds to the Realm of Darkness, utters a resounding cry (Khrōshtag) to Ohrmizd, who catches it and returns an answer (Padvākhtag). [55] Ohrmizd is liberated, but he has to leave behind his armor, the Five Elements, in the power of the enemy. However, they become the undoing of the Powers of Darkness, a bait, which they cannot digest. But they are still captives. Therefore, in order to secure a permanent liberation of the various particles of Light, they strike a decisive blow at the Powers of Darkness; and heaven and earth are created out of their dead bodies, "the captive bodies of the tribe of darkness" (*de captivis corporibus gentis tenebrarum*, *Contra Faustum* 20:9). From the particles of Light completely unaffected by darkness, sun and moon are created, from those contaminated to a slight degree, the stars. Thus only a third, apparently hopelessly corrupt mass of Light is left behind. In order to release it the world must be set in motion. A third evocation of deities then takes place (the Third Messenger (Tertius legatus, Rōshnshahr), Jesus (Khradēshahr), the Maiden of Light). The Third Messenger sets the world in motion after the Living Spirit's five sons have had their special tasks assigned to them. [56] Thus a kind of machine for the liberation of Light has been provided. Through an extremely complicated process of purification the particles of Light now may be conveyed farther and farther up, along the Column of Glory to the moon and the sun, in order finally to enter purified into paradise. This process frightens the Powers of Darkness out of their wits, and in a desperate attempt at preserving some of the captive particles of Light, the first human couple, Gēhmurd and Murdiyānag, Adam and Eve, are created. Through them and their descendents, the demons of darkness hope that they can preserve some Light. Man is created in the image of the Third Messenger and thus is rooted in both worlds; but man is not conscious of his high descent. The necessary knowledge, *Gnōsis*, is missing. The work of redemption therefore must be concentrated on man.

Through the imparting of knowledge all Light bound in matter must be saved. And this process will go on until, after the Great War and Fire and Judgement, the restoration takes place. And still, according to the severe emphasis laid by the Manichaeans on the power of sin and its disastrous consequences, the possibility exists that part of the Light, part of God himself, may be forfeited with the souls of the damned and be imprisoned with the demonic powers in the large "close-knit lump" *(bōlos, globus)*. Mani admits that Darkness can corrupt that which is homomorphic *(hāmchihrag)*, viz. with Light, with God to such a degree that it can no longer be called homomorphic. He thus assumes an idea of predestination fatally illogical for the coherence of the doctrine. But still the designation of that which is struck by the definitive destruction is "that Power of Light"! Augustine drew that conclusion mercilessly and without extenuating additions, even adducing the Manichaeans' own statements:

> And not only so, but they do not (even) hesitate to say that he (God) will punish even his own limbs together with that tribe (i.e., the tribe of Darkness) [*Contra Adimantum* VII, 1].
>
> And what could not be purified of God's own part, is at the end of the world bound with an eternal penal chain [*Epistola* CCXXXVI, 2].
>
> But what end is there? What other end than that God has been unable to purify everything (viz. divine) [*Contra Felicem Manichaeum* II, 7].

This train of thought, which in its almost blasphemous boldness is unparalleled in the history of religion, categorically prevents any attempt at a development towards grotesque libertinism. It has spread unrest and confusion and given a cheap material for odious attacks to superficial controversialists, but its place in Manichaean theology is logically connected with fundamental elements in Mani's anthropology.

On the Five Greatnesses

... [the 12 Aeons who stand] before the Great King, God Zurvān. The third, the Blessed Places (i.e., the Aeons of the Aeons) without count and number, wherein dwell the Light Gods, Angels, Elements, and Powers in great bliss and joy.

The fourth, the Pure Air (i.e., *aër ingenitus*) in the Light Paradise, wondrous, beautiful to behold, immeasurable its goodness for them. By supernatural power it shall, by itself, bring into being the god's marvellous dress and garment, throne, diadem, and fragrant wreath, ornaments, and finery of all kinds.

The fifth, the Light Earth (i.e., *terra ingenita*), *self-existent, eternal, miraculous; in *height it is beyond *reach (?), its *depth cannot be perceived. No enemy and no *injurer walk this Earth. Its divine pavement is of the substance of diamond that does not shake for ever. All good things are born from it: adorned, graceful hills wholly covered with flowers, grown in much excellence; green fruit-bearing trees whose fruits never *drop, never rot, and never become wormed; springs flowing with ambrosia that fill the whole Paradise, its groves and plains; countless mansions and palaces, thrones and *benches that exist in perpetuity for ever and ever.

Thus arranged is the Paradise, in these Five Greatnesses. They are calm in quietude and know no fear. They live in the light, where they have no darkness; in eternal life, where they have no death; in health without sickness; in joy, where they have no sorrow; in charity without hatred; in the company of friends, where they have no separation; in a shape that is not brought to naught, in a divine body where there is no destruction; on ambrosial food without restriction, wherefore they bear no toil and hardship. In appearance they are ornate, in strength powerful, in wealth exceedingly rich; of poverty they know not even the name. Nay, they are equipped, beautiful, and embellished; no damage occurs to their bodies. Their garment of joy is finery that never gets soiled, of seventy myriad kinds, set with jewels. Their places are never destroyed...

[M 178 I = I B 4990 I, Sogdian: W.B. Henning, "A Sogdian Fragment of the Manichaean Cosmogony," *BSOAS* 12 (1948): 307 ff.; *Cat.* p. 143]

The Father of Greatness

... for that reason that He is a great sovereign in battle and full of love; He it is who was [not over]come by the enemy, for that reason that He ... a friend; He it is over whom no foul smell came, for that reason that He is all ... fragrance; He it is who was not seized by death, for that reason that He is all life.

[M 102 R 1-8, Parthian: *HR* II: 64; *Cat.* p. 9]

12 diadems of Light He has, and before Him stand the 12 Great Ones, His sons, 12 of the same kind, the brilliant form of the Father of Light; the many gods, divinities and Jewels of the train of the Sovereign of Paradise He created, called forth and placed, and besides those the twelve Great First-born Giants and Sovereigns ...

His great glory they always bless and praise, the merciful God, the righteous God, truly with joy ...

.   .   .   .

Counsel and instruction He gave His sons that they perfect and finish ...

.   .   .   .

the powerful one, the highest of the Gods, Lord of the magnates, the most divine of the divinities. Praise upon God, the glory of the Lights, the high Light of the blessed realm where you dwell, pure and brilliant, beautiful and gentle, wholly full of joy, peace and trust, eternal life ... fragrance.

[From M 730, Parthian: W.-L. II: 553-54; *Cat.* p. 49.]

[All divinities] and gods were evoked [and established] by Him (i.e., the Father of Greatness); all rejoice in Him and to Him [give] praise. The Land of Light... through its five pure Thoughts; it is fragrant with sweet winds, it shines in every region. Powers, divinities and gods, Jewels and joyous Aeons, trees, fountains and plants rejoice in Him day by day. The [measureless?] living sea ... clothed through Him ...

[M 533 II, Parthian: Mary Boyce, "Some Parthian Abecedarian Hymns," *BSOAS* 14 (1952): pp. 443-44; *Cat.* p. 38]

The Realm of Light and the Realm of Darkness

(a) And not ange[r, not greed]
    and not lust, not ...
    and not trick, not ...
    and not ..., not harm
    and not turmoil, not pillage
    and not sin, not hunger
    and not thirst, not coldness
    and not heat, not grief
    and not sorrow, not pain
    and not sickness, not old age
    and not death, not from ...
    and not even hate (?) ...
    and fortunate ...
    happy is he who ...

(b) ... and also that
   ... that Ahrmēn and
   [[the devil]s had carried on a battle
   in the five caves (i.e., the five parts of the Realm of Darkness),
                                                          [and one
   was deeper than the other.
   And that Āz (Greed),
   the mother of the devils, from whom
   all sin has gone out,
   (she) from the five caves
   with the five poisonous springs
   and the five tastes
   [... sal]ty, sour,
   [sharp (i.e., burnt), sweet] and bitter
   ... with five ...

   [M 183 I, Parthian: Ed. W. Sundermann, lines 1174-1202; *Cat.* p. 14]

The Prince of Darkness

The hideous demon ... and the form ...
He scorches, he destroys ... he terrifies ...
He flies upon wings, as a being of air; he swims with fins like
   one of the water; and he crawls like those of the darkness.
He is with armour on (his) four limbs, as when the children
   of the fire run against him in the manner of the beings of hell.
Poisonous springs gush from him; and from him are breathed
   out [smoky] fogs; he shakes (?) (his) teeth [like] daggers.

. . . .

... through ... and hideousness.
... they ... one another ... tyranny of perdition.
They are rotting upon a couch of darkness; in pursuit of desire
   and in lust they bear and again destroy one another.
The quarrelsome Prince of Darkness has subdued those five
   pits of destruction (i.e., the five regions oi the Realm of
   Darkness), through great ... (?) terror and wrath.
He has flung much poison and wickedness from that deep
   upon ... and it (?) stood ... through ....

   [M 507, Parthian: Mary Boyce, op. cit., pp. 441-42; *Cat.* p. 36]

The First Man

The righteous God, the Highest of the Gods,
who diadem and eternal glory ...
was proud and glad, (he), the blissful one amongst the Lights,
when you (i.e., the First Man) were born in the realm.
The twelve sons and the Aeons of the Aeons
of the *aër ingenitus* were happy-minded.
All gods and inhabitants (of the Realm),
the mountains, the trees, and the springs,
the wide, strong palaces and halls
became glad-minded through you, Friend.
When the lovely maidens and girls.
sprung from Sense (i.e., one of the five limbs), saw you,
they all unanimously with praise
blessed you, Faultless Youth.
Tambourine, harp and flute sounded,
music of songs from all sides.
All gods were in front
of you, Prince, son of a king.
Voices sound from the *aër ingenitus*,
music of songs from the Light-Earth (i.e., *ṭerra ingenita*),
as they say thus to the Father of Light:
The battle-stirrer has been born who makes peace.
For ever all-good, the Highest of the Gods
has entrusted you with three tasks:
Destroy death, smite the enemies,
and cover the whole Paradise of Light!
You paid homage and went out for battle
and covered the whole Paradise of Light.
The tyrannic prince was bound for ever and ever,
and the dwelling-place of the Dark Ones was destroyed.
The Light Friend, the First Man
was (stayed) there, until he has carried out the Fathers' will.

[M 10, R 11- V 22, Parthian: Walter Henning, "Geburt und Entsendung des manichäischen Urmenschen," *NGWG*, 1933, p. 306 ff.; *Cat.* p. 2]

... like a humble shepherd among wild animals, a helmsman in the middle of the roughness of the sea, like a sovereign in the middle of fight and battle. And they (the Mother of the Living and the Living Spirit) sent Khvandag (lit. "called," here the Call, Cry, Khrōshtag, the divinized cry of salvation) to him (i.e., the First Man), as one shoots a letter with an arrow into a town. Quickly, [in] haste he came down [like] a big rock (thrown) into the sea.

[From M 819, Middle Persian: Ed. W. Sundermann, lines 797-805; *Cat.* p. 55]

And (like) a hero whose arrow does not bring perdition in traps (?), but turns against attackers and commanders, so God Ohrmizd keeps the Five Lights (= the Five Elements of Light, his sons, viz. ether, wind, light, water, fire). And he ... threw them like fodder before the demons and ... before the oxen. And when the demons ... to the fire, then it rose up ... .
Then he seized the demons through the Five Lights. And God Ohrmizd went out to the dark earth like a lion against a mighty ... and (like) a powerful attacker against the fortress of the enemies. And he cut up the demons and seized the dark earth as a point (seizes) a ..., an axe a ... (and) a powerful attacker a fortress. And for a long t[ime] he was in there. And he ... the enemies ...

[From M 316 and M 801 d, Parthian: Ed. W. Sundermann, lines 938-947 and 950-959; *Cat.* p. 22 and 54]

And that First-born (i.e., here the First Man, otherwise usually about Jesus,) offspring of the Aeons and First Head, shone and appeared in beautiful form amongst all these powers like a light star amongst the dark ones and like a human being amongst wild animals and like a god amongst demons. Thus that God, [the First] Man, appeared. And again, to all these powers it (i.e., the Light) was like a sweet meal before hungry ones: When it stands before them, they all devour it.

[From the fragments M 1001, M 1012, M 1013, and M 1015, Middle Persian: Ed. W. Sundermann, lines 113-133; *Cat.* p. 63]

For pity ... he (i.e., the First Man) put on the body ... . The first garb of the [God] Ohrmizd; when (he) had clothed the enemies in (his) five sons, he gave (his) soul to the darkness; he surrendered his own soul; he loosened (his) limbs for the

sake of the sons. He tied up the enemies; he revived (his) sons
and with gentleness saved the kingdom. ... there came this
beneficent father (i.e., probably the Living Spirit) [with his]
brethren, and saved his own Light. [He that] understood,
(and) recalled all: the first, the middle and the last things
(i.e., *initium, medium, finis*, the period of the unwounded Light,
of the mixture and of the salvation), (his) lips and tongue
responded and spoke with great praises, with ... mouth. He
revealed the path of salvation and the pure road [to all] souls
who were in harmony. No more the worlds wait (in vain) and
... for the wished-for good. and those pure ... .

[From M 710 and M 5877, Parthian: Mary Boyce, "Some Parthian Abecedarian Hymns, " *BSOAS*, vol. 14, no. 3 (1952): 445-46; *Cat*, p. 47 and 116]

THE PRAYER OF THE MOTHER OF THE RIGHTEOUS
THE BATTLE OF GOD OHRMIZD

[And when] the wind-devils understood that ..., then all,
like a hard cohort, [57] jointly fell over him in the Wind Land
(i.e., the realm of the dark wind in the middle of the Realm of
Darkness). Then God Ohrmizd prayed to his mother, and his
mother prayed to the Righteous God: "Send a helper to my
son, for he has carried out your will, and he has come into
oppression." ...

Swiftly God [Khrōshtag] descended, and he split up the cohort
of the devils, and gave him (i.e., God Ohrmizd) greetings
from the Father and from the whole Realm (of Light). He said:
"Collect your limbs (i.e., be prepared for salvation), for your
redeemer has come." And God Ohrmizd rejoiced at the joyful
good news, and he created God Padvākhtag. And both went
up ... the Mother of the Righteous, Padvākhtag ... .

[M 21, Parthian: *MM* III: 890-91; *Cat*. p. 3]

Gods and Devils of the Manichaean Cosmogony

... and not to Hell, where they shall not find refreshment
either, until their defeat comes.

. . . .

And when Mihr[yazd] (God Mihr, i.e., the Living Spirit,

as always in Middle Persian texts; in Parthian texts = the Third Messenger) had made and arranged those four layers (lit. downward-leadings, i.e., the lower parts of the earths), the prison of the demons, and four earths (i.e., the four upper ones) with columns and arrangements and gates and walls and ditches and hells and the canals that are in the womb of the earth, and mountains and valleys and springs, rivers and seas, and 10 heavens with climes and thrones and provinces and houses and villages and tribes and lands and boundaries and watch- posts and gates, thresholds (i.e., months), revolutions (i.e., days) and double hours and walls, and one celestial sphere with the signs of the zodiac and the stars, and two chariots, (that) of the sun and (that of) the moon, with houses and thrones and gates and door-keeper leaders, and the Lord of the Prison and the Lord of the Watch-post, the Lord of the House and the Lord of the Village, the Lord of the Tribe and the Lord of the Country, and all sorts of things of the universe, then this Envoy-and Messenger-God whom Mihryazd and the female-formed (god), the Mother-of-the-God-Ohrmizd, had ... above his body, (and) ... were placed there before that [god] (i.e., the Splenditenens) who stands above that firmament and holds the head(s) of those gods (i.e., the Elements).

. . . .

And Mihryazd and the female-formed creator were led up to Paradise. And together with God Ohrmizd (i.e., the First Man) and the Sweetest One of the Lights (i.e., the Friend of the Lights) and the New-World-Maker-God (i.e., the Great Builder) they stood, saluting, before the Sovereign of Paradise. And they prostrated themselves and paid deep homage and spoke thus: "You, the Lord, we show reverence, (you) who called us forth through your miraculous power and your word of blessing. And through us you bound Āz (Greed) and Ahrmēn and the demons and the witches."

. . . .

"Order (him) (i.e., the new god whom the Sovereign is asked to call forth) that he shall go and observe the prison of the demons and apportion sun and moon revolution and tending (viz. of the Elements of Light) and become liberator and savior of

that Goodness and Light of God (i.e., the particles of Light in
the material world) that from the beginning was struck by Āz
and Ahrmēn and the demons and the witches, and that they also
now keep oppressed, and also of that one (i.e., the part of the
Goodness and Light of God in water, plants, etc.) that is kept
in the climes of earth and heaven and endures wretchedness,
and (that he shall) prepare road and path to the Highest for
the wind, water and fire."

Then the Sovereign of Paradise through his wonder-working
power and his word of blessing evoked three gods: Rōshnshahr
(i.e., the God "whose Realm is Light," the Third Messenger)
and Khradēshahr (i.e.,the God "whose Realm is Wisdom,"
Jesus; the third god, not mentioned, must be the Maiden of
Light) (to take care) of the leading upwards (viz. of the Light),
so that, just as the Lord himself is Sovereign of Paradise and
holds all his Light, so also that God Rōshnshahr can have
lordship and rulership over earth and heaven and hold the
Light of the universe and make day and night appear, and God
Khradēshahr ... that Light and Goodness (of God) that after ...

[T III 260 e II = M 7984 II, Middle Persian: *MM* I: 177-81; *Cat.* p. 133]

Plants, flowers and herbs and plants without seeds and all sorts
of growing things were sown and grew up; and into them Āz
mixed her own Self. And that one part that had fallen into the
sea, from that there became one hideous, cruel and terrible
Mazan (i.e., "monster," a kind of demon); and he tottered
out of the sea and began sinning in the world.

.   .   .   .

Then Mihryazd sent out from (amongst) those five gods (i.e.,
his five sons) of his own evocation that one Four-formed God
(i.e., Light-Adamas) that stretched out this Mazan over the
whole north from east to west in the northern district, thrust
his foot into him and threw him down and stood upon him,
so that he could not sin in the world. And this god (Adamas)
he(i.e., Mihryazd) made Lord of the Village over the [uni]verse,
of earth [and heaven, over the North and] the East, the South
and the West so that he could protect the world. And like that
lewd and phallophoric (?) (monster) Āz fell from heaven
to earth in dry and moist (places), and she ... in all sorts of

weeds and demons (lit. mazan) of her own essence (self).

. . . .

Then these demons and witches, demons of wrath, Mazans and Asrēshtārs (i.e., a class of demons, otherwise unknown) that were female — the two-legged and four-legged and winged and poisonous and reptile-shaped (beings), all that in the beginning were pregnant from hell and thereafter had been bound in the 11 (otherwise 10!) heavens and had seen that splendor and beauty of God Rōshnshahr and become greedy after him and (thereafter) unconscious — then their offspring was miscarried from them. And they (i.e., the abortions) came down to the earth and began to rise on the earth. And they devoured the fruits and the fruit from the trees and grew bigger and became Mazan and Asrēshtār. And from the fruits and the fruit of the the trees, Āz (Greed) came upon them; and in lust they were excited and had intercourse together.

Then God Rōshnshahr ordered the New-World-Maker-God (= the Great Builder): "Go and then build the New Building aside from the universe of earth and heaven and outside those five hells, towards the southern region, from there still further away across the hell of Darkness, from the East up to the western region, like Paradise. And make in the middle of this building a firm prison for Āz and Ahrmēn and the demons and the witches. And hereafter, when that Light and Goodness of God that was swallowed by Ahrmēn and the demons and (now) is tortured and writhes in all climes and in the demons and the witches, when then that (Light and Goodness of God) is made pure and is drawn up to the Highest, and Frashēgird (i.e., the final Restoration) comes, then Āz and Ahrmēn and the demons and the witches shall be bound for ever and ever, without end in that prison.

"And make, above that New Building, the New Paradise, so that it (can be) a throne and ... for Ohrmizd and these Gods (i.e., the five Elements of Light) that because of their miraculous power and light had been seized and bound by Āz and Ahrmēn and the demons and the witches, and (also) for us ... ."

[T III 260 b I = M 7981 I, Middle Persian: *MM* I: 181(85; *Cat.* p. 133]

Another version of Light-Adamas' victory over the monster:

... like a gazelle to the hunting ground. And he laid it down, its head in the East, its feet in the West, between four mountains, its waist in the North, its face towards the South, like a lion in the pitfall (?). His left foot [he placed] on its breast and its neck, his right foot on [its thigh] ... .

[M 292 V II, 1-9, Middle Persian: *MM* I; 182, note 2; *Cat.* p. 21]

... through wisdom [and] knowledge ... body great, the creation of ether and after (the creation of) ether (that of) wind and after (the creation of) wind (that of) light and after (the creation of) light (that of) water and after (the creation of) water the creation of fire. And he (i.e., Ohrmizd) put them (i.e., the five Elements of Light) on as a garment and had the fire in his hand. And he went for Ahrmēn and the demons and smote them and defeated them.

And ... wind ... and ... shall arrange, and water shall purify fire. And they shall always be together, having the same mind and the same power. And that first Light and Goodness of their own those Elements (i.e., wind, water, and fire) have under their own protection, and they fulfilled the will of God Ohrmizd.

· · · · · · · · · · · · · · · ·

When then God Rōshnshahr had placed this World-Holder-God (i.e., probably the Column of Glory) in the middle of the universe and arranged these gods, then further God Rōshnshahr (and) the Female-formed God and God Ohrmizd with his own origin and ... these gods [and] that chariot ... were placed in the chariots of the sun and moon in order that that Light and Goodness of God which in the beginning was chewed and devoured by Āz and the demons and the witches, male and female ones, and which they also now keep caught, and also that (Light) which they until Frashēgird chew and [devour] from wind, water and fire ...

· · · · · · · · · · · · · · · ·

... was mixed with, when Ohrmizd and Ahrmēn were fighting with each other. And then he (i.e., the Third Messenger) by the help of the revolution and the tending of the sun and the moon and (of) the protection and the care of the gods leads that Light and Goodness (of God) up from the universe of earth and heaven and [guides] it to [Paradise]. ... day

... becomes ... And ... when it is in the fifteenth of the months, at full moon, (then) God Ohrmizd takes away that Light and Increase of the Moon God — in the god of his (i.e., Ohrmizd's) own origin — and arranges it. And from full moon, the sixteenth of the months, until new moon, the twenty[-ninth of the months] ...

. . . .

... ne[w moon] come together, [then] God Ohrmizd rises from the chariot of the Moon God and comes up to the chariot of the Sun. And these gods that God Ohrmizd, from full moon until new moon, day after day [leads] from the chariot of the Moon God to the chariot of the Sun ...

. . . .

... a month is counted and appears after thirty days and after (appearing) new moon and full moon and disappearing (lit. invisible) moon.

And that Āz and Ahrmēn and darkness and dimness and the parching wind that (is) of evil smell, and the poison of death and the angry burning and the poison of the demons and ...

[T III 260 a = M 7980, Middle Persian: *MM* I: 185-88; *Cat.* p. 132]

THE SPEECH ON GĒHMURD (AND) MURDIYĀNAG

... (away from ?) Ahrmēn and the demons, up from the universe he will first draw (them) and lead (them) to the sun and the moon and to Paradise, his own [family]. And then the universe will become Frashēgird (i.e., the final Renewal). And the defeat (?) of Āz and the demons will come; and the sun and the moon and the gods will find halt and rest.

. . . .

And also in the beginning, when the gods had distributed zones, places and frontiers according to the revolution and the protecting control and the waxing and the waning of the sun and the moon and made day and night and month and year visible, and (when) they purified Light out of the universe, then this Āz of defeated offspring, Āz, who had fallen down from the sky and put on trees and plants as a garment and by the help of the trees and the plants put on as a garment the abortions of the Mazans and Asrēshtārs that had fallen down from the

sky — and by them that splendor and nobleness of [God]
Narisah (i.e., the Third Messenger) was ... and was seen ...
yes, thereupon she (Āz) observed the sun and the moon giving
protection; and likewise she saw the god(s) and the sun and
the moon continuously releasing (lit. make pure) also that
Goodness and Light of God that she (i.e., Āz) has captured
from (the bondage of) Greed and (up) from the universe and
leading it, protected, to the chariots and transporting it to
Paradise.

Then that tricked Āz was filled with heavy anger. She began
to desire (to make) a step (forward), and she thought: "After
those two forms — the female and the male — of God Narisah
that I have seen, I will form those two creatures, the male and
the female, so that they become my garment and veil. ... by me
these [two creatures] shall not be taken away, and I will let no
misery and wretchedness come [over them]." Thereupon the
Āz from all that progeny of the demons that had fallen down
unto the earth from the sky put on as a garment these (two),
the male Asrēshtār and the female Asrēshtār, lion-shaped, lustful
and wrathful, sinful and terrible. She made them her own veil
and garment and raged within them. And just as the Āz herself
from the (primeval) beginning in that hell of Darkness, her
abode, had taught the demons and witches, the demons of wrath,
the Mazans and Asrēshtārs, male and female, lewdness and
copulation, so again thereafter Āz began to teach also these,
the other male and female Mazans and Asrēshtārs that had
fallen unto the earth from the sky, lewdness and copulation so
that they might become lewd and copulate and, with joined
bodies, be mixed together and (so that) dragon progeny might
be born from them, and (so that) Āz (then) might take and
devour that progeny in order to make herefrom two creatures,
a man and a woman.

Then this Mazan and Asrēshtār, the male and the female,
taught all (the others) lewdness and copulation. And they were
mixed together, with joined bodies. And their progeny was
born and fostered. And they gave their own progeny to these
two Asrēshtārs, the male and the female, lion-shaped, the
garment of Āz, and full of lust. And Āz devoured that progeny
and made these two Mazans, the male and the female, lewd

and made them copulate, and they were mixed together, with joined bodies. And that mixture which they from that progeny of Mazans and Asrēshtārs which she devoured, had put on as a garment, that (mixture) she formed by her own lasciviousness and made one body of male form, with bones, sinews, flesh, veins and skin.

And (part) of that Light and Goodness of God that through (lit. from) fruits and buds was mixed with that progeny of Mazans, was bound into this body as a soul. And in it (i.e., the body of the first man) was inserted their greed and lust, salaciousness and copulation and enmity and calumny, envy and sinfulness, wrath and impurity, ... and senselessness and wickedness of soul and doubt, stealing and lying, robbery and ill-doing, obstinacy (?) and ..., revenge and .... sorrow and grief, pain and tooth-ache, poverty and begging, illness and old age, stench and brigandage (?).

And those various words and voices of these Mazan abortions from which that body was built, she (Āz) gave to this creature (i.e., the first man) that he might speak and understand the varied words.

And that male descendant of the gods that (came) from the chariot (and) was seen by her, exactly after him (with him as a model) she formed and built it (the first man). And also from above, from the sky, she joined for him binding and connection with the Mazans and the Asrēshtārs and the zodiac and the planets so that upon him might rain wrath, lust and sinfulness from the Mazans and the zodiac, and so that the will might penetrate him to become more cruel and more Mazan-like, greedy and lustful. And when that male creature had been born, then she gave it the name of the "first man," namely Gēhmurd. And then those two Asrēshtārs, the male and the female, lion-shaped, again ate from the very same progeny of their friends and they were penetrated by lewdness and copulation, and they were mixed together, with joined bodies. And Āz, who had filled them from that progeny of the Mazans that they ate, she again in the same way formed and built another body, a female one, with bones, sinews, flesh, veins and skin."

[T III 260 e I = M 7984, and T III 260 c = M 7982 ,Middle Persian: *MM* I: 191-97; *Cat.* p. 133]

"And after that Female-formed descendant of the Gods(i.e., the Maiden of Light) that (came) from the chariot (and) was seen by her (the Āz), so she had formed and built her (i.e., the first woman). And (also) for her, from the sky she joined binding and connection with the zodiac and the planets so that also upon her might rain wrath, lewdness and sinfulness from the Mazans and the zodiac, and so that the will might penetrate her to become more cruel and more sinful, filled with lewdness and lust, and so that she might deceive this man through lust, and so that from these two creatures mankind might be born in the world, and so that they might become greedy and lustful and behave (lit. go) wrathfully and maliciously and mercilessly, and so that they might strike water and fire, trees and plants and worship greed and lust, do what the demons want, and go to hell.

Thereafter, when that female creature had been born, then they gave her the name of the "Female of Glories," namely Murdiyānag. And when those two creatures, the male and the female, had been born in the world and fostered and had become older, then great joy came to Āz and to the Asrēshtārs of the demons. And this leader of the Asrēshtārs made a gathering of the Mazans and the Asrēshtārs. He said to these two human beings: "For your sake I have created the earth and the sky, the sun and the moon, water and fire, trees and plants (and) wild and tame animals so that you thereby might become joyful and happy and glad and do my will." And a dragon, Mazan and terrible, he set over these two children as a guard (thinking): "He shall protect them and not allow anybody to lead them away from us. For these Mazans and Asrēshtārs fear the gods and are afraid that they should come over us and strike us or bind us. For these two children have been formed and built after the appearance and form of the gods."

As thereafter that "first man" and (that) "Female of Glories," the first man and the first woman, began ruling over the earth, then greed was awakened in them. And wrath penetrated them, and they began filling up springs, striking trees and plants, and ruling, in very great wrath (?), over the earth, and becoming greedy. And the gods they do not fear. And these five Elements of Light (lit. Amahrāspands) through which the world has been arranged they do not recognize, but hurt incessantly.

[From T III 260 d I = M 7983, Middle Persian: MM I: 198-201; *Cat.* p. 133]

The myth alluded to in this text is the well-known myth about the seduction of the demons by the Third Messenger or the Maiden of Light (*virgo, parthénos,* Sadvēs) or, without any specific difference, according to the Manichaean principle of identity, the twelve Maidens of Light (also named the Beautiful Girls (*Contra Faustum* 20:6), *virtutes (lucis)* (*De natura boni* 44), and Zurvān's twelve Radiant Daughters (in the Zoroastrian polemical writing *Shkand gumānik vichār* 16: 31). These arouse the lust of the demons by appearing in a male shape before the females and in female shape before the males in order, by their shedding of semen, to release the Light swallowed by them. As a consequence of this episode and also as a countermove, Āz, with the male and female Asrēshtār as instruments, effects the creation of man in the image of the Third Messenger. The motif utilized, the vanquishing of an opponent by giving rise to sexual desire, is by no means unknown in the ancient Orient. Its use in Zoroastrianism or especially Zurvanism was hardly without importance for the Manichaean elaboration, the more so as Narsa, Nēryōsang, who is presented in his nakedness in order to arouse the desire of women, in the Middle Persian (God Narisah) and Parthian (God Narisaf) texts denotes the Third Messenger.

The myth was maliciously utilized and met with disgust by the attackers of Manichaeism. Especially the manner of the creation of Adam caused horror:

Any one believing that the first man, called Adam, was not made by God, but was generated by the Princes of Darkness, to the end that the portion of God *(pars dei)* which was held captive in their members might be found in more abundant plenty in the world, let him be cursed (anathema).

[The big Latin abjuration formula (*Prosperi Anathematismi* 4), Alfred Adam, *Texte zum Manichaismus* (Berlin, 1954), p. 91.]

The Manichaeans' own detailed accounts of the matter show its not inessential significance in their cosmogony and corroborate the polemists' rendering of it. But while, to the latter, it was not much more than a collection of obscenities, it was to the Manichaeans a "Jacob story," which showed God's wisdom and foresight.

Other Manichaean Texts

He (presumably the Third Messenger) takes the Light away from it (the world) in many forms and fashions; by gentle means and harsh, he releases the captives from bondage. He purifies his own life, and encourages them to move after the apparition and to follow the form. Bright Sadvēs shows her form to the Demon of Wrath; by her own (nature) she seduces him.[58] He thinks she is the essence (of Light). He sows ... he groans when he no longer sees the form. Light is born in the sphere: she gives it to the higher Powers. The dirt and dross flows from him to the earth. It clothes itself in all phenomena, and is reborn in many fruits. The dark Demon of Wrath is ashamed, for he was distraught and had become naked. He had not attained to the higher, and had been bereft of what he had achieved. He left the body an empty shell and descended in shame. He covered himself in the womb of the earths, whence he had risen in brutishness. Lo, the great kingdom of redemption awaits on high, ready for those who Know, so that they find peace therein at last.

The sinful, dark Pēsūs (i.e., the female Asrēshtār) runs hither and thither in brutishness; to the upper and the lower limbs she gives no peace at all. She seizes, she binds the Light in the six great bodies: in earth water and fire, wind plants and animals. She fashions it in many shapes, she moulds it in many figures; she fetters it in a prison, that it may not mount up on high. She weaves on all sides, she builds up; she sets a Watcher over it. Greed and Lust were made its fellow-captives. She mixed destructive air into those six great bodies. She builds up her own body, but destroys the sons of those. The Light Powers above discomfit all demons of wrath, the sons of that Pēsūs, who is in a higher place.

[From M 741, Parthian: Mary Boyce, "Sadwēs and Pēsūs," *BSOAS*, vol. 13 no. 4 (1951): 911 ff.; *Cat.* p. 49]

Angry became Āz,
that evil mother of all demons,
and she made a heavy disturbance
for the sake of helping herself.
And of the dirt (?) of the demons
and of the filth of the she-demons
she made this body,
and she herself entered it.
Then from the five Elements of Light (lit. Amahrāspands),
the armor of Lord Ohrmizd,
she formed (?) the good soul
and fettered it into the body.
She made it (i.e., the first man) like one blind and deaf,
unconscious and deceived.
that he at first might not know
his (true) origin and family.
She (Āz) created the body and prison,
and fettered the grieved [59] soul:
"And my jailers are robbers,
demons, she-demons, and all witches!"
Firmly she fettered the soul
into the fraudulent body;
and she made it hateful and evil,
angry and vengeful.
Then Lord Ohrmizd
had mercy on the souls,
and in human form
he came down to the earth.
He (i.e., Ohrmizd) maimed the evil Āz;
and he made obvious
and clearly showed (man)
everything that has been and will be.
Swiftly he revealed
that this body of flesh
was not made by Lord Ohrmizd,
nor was the soul itself fettered by him.
The wise soul of the fortunate one
was (given) resurrection;

he believed in the Knowledge
of Ohrmizd, the Good Lord.
All injunction and orders
and seals of the Peacefulness (i.e., Mani's religion)
he accepted to the greatest extent,
like an active hero.
He put off the body of death
. and was for ever saved;
and he ascended into Paradise,
into that land of the blessed."

[From S 9, Leningrad, Middle Persian: C. Salemann, "Manichaica III," *Bulletin de l'Académie Impériale des Sciences de St.-Pétersbourg*, 1912, pp. 9 and 18; Walter Henning, "Ein manichäischer kosmogonischer Hymnus," *NGWG*, 1932, p. 215 ff.]

And he (i.e., the Living Spirit) prepared two chariots, each with five walls. Of pure Fire and Light he prepared the chariot of the Sun. And in every single wall he put twelve gates. And in all there are sixty gates. And then he prepared the chariot of the Moon from Wind and immortal Water. And in every single wall he put fourteen gates. And in all there are seventy gates. Then he ... the Five Light ... placed five angels (i.e., the five soul-gathering angels) in the chariot of the Sun and five in the Moon.

[From M 183 II, Parthian: Ed. W. Sundermann, lines 1207-1227; *Cat.* p. 14]

And God Mihr (the Living Spirit) laid the foundations of all worlds like an architect who carries through a construction and has employed workers. ... they bring; and he himself piles up and builds the whole construction of this palace with mastery; and thus he with craftmanship divides that palace into room after room.

[M 100 R III, 7-24 ,Middle Persian: Ed. W. Sundermann, lines 705-722; *Cat.* p. 89]

... mat]ter is distributed which (in) itself is seven she-demons: The first one is the skin, the second one the flesh, the third one the vein(s), the fourth one the blood, the fifth one the sinews, the sixth ...

[From M 1005, Middle Persian: Ed. W. Sundermann, lines 363-368; *Cat.* p. 63]

(... she (i.e., Greed, Āz) took. And she made this carrion, the microcosm *(shahr īg qōdak)*, in order to be made joyful through it. And she filled it throughout with deception and fading and disagreement, for in her great carrion many powers are exceedingly deceitful.

[From the fragments M 1002, M 1017, and M 1028, Middle Persian: Ed. W. Sundermann, lines 456-465; *Cat.* p. 63-64]

From the Last Chapter of an Eschatological Work

And then the battle-stirring gods lead and guide their Aeons and those homomorphic (with them) (i.e., the unhurt parts of the Living Self) that they had called into the Great Earth (i.e., probably, a lower part of the New Paradise) and placed (there), by divine proclamation to the New Aeon (i.e., the New Paradise), and settle there in the same way as nomads who (going) from place to place with their tents, horses and possessions, put up and pull down (their tents).

But that power of Light that is so mixed with Darkness that it cannot be separated from it again, yes, that is not homomorphic (or consubstantial, sc. with what is guided to the New Paradise), for that reason that it from the beginning foresaw: "So (it is) for me, because it was determined to be (so)!" And therefore it is not called homomorphic. And further, those (parts of the) five (Elements of Light) in battle prayed to God Ohrmizd: "Do not leave us in the body of Darkness, but send us power and a helper." And God Ohrmizd promised them: "I will not abandon you to the Powers of Darkness!" In that case it was not the power that knew: "For me the mixing with Darkness in the beginning reaches an injury and heaviness so wretched that I cannot be taken away and separated from Darkness." No, that was the power of Light that knew: "My mixture is of such a kind that I can be purified and saved by the help of God Ohrmizd and (his) brothers." And they did not pray for that reason that (they thought that) if they did not pray, then God Ohrmizd would not help them. But (it came) to them on account of that prayer! And the hope and promise of God Ohrmizd increased (their) power in the same way as (in the case of) fighters whose power increases through the zeal put on by the voice and heart of their friends.

And the gods will not be sorrowful because of that bit of Light that is mixed with Darkness and cannot be separated (from it), for sorrow is not characteristic of them. On the contrary, through the peace and joy that is radically characteristic of them, through (the fact) that they are joyous and (also) for that reason that they have subdued and bound Ahrmēn together with the enmity. And for a short while they clothed themselves inwardly with the costume of joy, but outwardly they were visible in armed (and) warlike appearance. And after that they have bound him in a prison of oblivion, and they themselves are ruling over it, then they are joyous, proud and happy; because (now) nobody can any longer do them harm.

And when all the battle-stirrers have rested for a short while in the New Aeon, and when also that little bit of the Light Earth and its mountains (?), wherefrom means for building the New Aeon had been taken, has been restored (lit. has come to its own measure), and when also the Last Man (i.e., the Light that has remained unliberated until the end of the world) stands (there) as the mightiest in stature, and when the warlike gods together with the five Lights have been healed from (their) wounds, then all the Jewels, the apostles, and the battle-stirring gods stand up and appear before the Sovereign of Paradise with imploring and prayer: First God Ohrmizd together with the Last Man, the Mother of the Righteous, the Friend of the Light(s), God Narisaf (i.e., the Third Messenger), God Bām (i.e., the Great Builder), the Living Spirit, Jesus the Splendour, the Maiden of Light and the Great *Nous*, these Light Fathers together with their gods, apostles and Aeons, all (of them) rightly in one thought, with one praise, in one voice, in one word and in one wish.

They raise their voice in prayer and worship for the great Jewel Srōshāv (i.e., the Father of Greatness), the primeval, the righteous God, the highest of the gods, and they say: "You, you are the Father of Light, of primeval existence from eternity; and to your dominion there is no harm. And also that sinner who boasted deceitfully and fought with your Greatness has been seized and bound in an extraordinary tomb, out of which he can no longer go. And also the earth, the dwelling-place of the enemies, we have overthrown and filled up and above we have built the light fundament of the New Aeon. And for you there are no more enemies and rivals, but yours is the eternal victory. Come now and show mercy upon us: Uncover your bright figure, the loveliest of all sights, for us who are longing for turning to it (and) becoming glad and joyous through it; because we for a long time have been longing for it." Then the Sovereign of Paradise ...

[M 2 II, Parthian: *MM* III: 849-53; *Cat.* p. 2]

It is easy to imagine how painful the problem dealt with in the above text has been to the Manichaeans. It was the logical consequence of this part of their teaching. It is admirable that they dared to draw it! For all opponents of Mani's Religion it was *gefundenes Fressen*:

Any one believing that there is a portion of God *(partem dei)*, which it has been found impossible to set free and cleanse from the mixture with the race of Darkness *(de commixtione gentis tenebrarum)*, and that it (the portion of God) is damned and everlastingly fastened to the horrible globe [60] wherein the race of Darkness is fastened up, let him be cursed (anathema).

[*Prosperi Anathematismi* 7: Alfred Adam, op. cit., p. 92]

Hymns to the Third Messenger

Hymn to Narisaf Yazd

The darkness and dross exuded (?) by them you shake down to the world. The Yakshas and Demons become ashamed, but the Light was freed from bondage. You are lord, ruler and prince of this world of seven climes, and of the Powers. You convulse the world and all creation for the sake of the Kindred, that they may be redeemed. Kind...

. . . .

They go to the heaven of Light, where the gods dwell and are at peace. They receive as their nature the original splendor

of the radiant palace and are joyful. They put on the resplendent
garment, and live for ever in Paradise.

[M 737, Parthian: Mary Boyce, "Sadwēs and Pēsūs," *BSOAS*, vol .13 no. 4
(1951): 915; *Cat.* p. 49]

The morning-light (?) and dawn is come,
the radiant Light from the East;
imposingly has appeared
the sovereign God Narisah.

[T II D 66 (= M 5260), V 1-4, Middle Persian: *MM* I: 192, n. 6; *Cat.*
p. 106]

And praise of ... our father, the Righteous God: As by themselves they keep guard (or: live) in peace and joy in the highest
(world), and nobody gives them poor care, so, from their peace
and well-being, confidence and delight shall be prepared for
the whole holy Church.

[M 26 R, Middle Persian: W.B. Henning, "The Sogdian Texts of Paris,"
BSOAS 11 (1946): 723; cf. H.W. Bailey, "Arya Notes," *Studia Classica et
Orientalia Antonino Pagliaro oblata*, vol. 1 (Rome, 1969), p. 139; *Cat.* p. 3]

With much blessing be blessed the bright-faced Light-Realm-
God. You, Light-Realm-God, are my beloved, merciful God,
save me! From the twelve gates (of heaven) (your) banner
and sign and splendor became visible. Splendid is your form,
and extended (?) this your action. You are the judge in earth
and heaven, you yourself are the witness. All splendor you
radiate brightly in the whole world. From heaven the gates
(are) open, and bright, the splendor blazes up. In miraculous
power you were born, and you went forth as a helper to the
father of men. The sons of the depth of the earth take the
Light from heaven. All your pious wish was fulfilled (complete),
saved (are) the saved, the condemned condemned. The sons
of Darkness are conquered upon earth; the sons of Day,
awakened, praise you. You convulse earth and heaven ...

. . . .

... you showed mercy in ... you are wished for among the indi-
gent, you are for (giving) salvation, a treasure of jewels that
you collect, is theirs;[61] at all times you lead (your) sons up-
upwards. You are the Sovereign who gives as a present the

diadcm, thc banner and the white sign. You, you are the compassionate Sovereign, show also me compassion and pity. I will always declare your fame. Save also me, for I am feeble. Blessed among days (be) this day, when the Son of God descended to the earth. On this day the assembly of the apostles — blessed be for ever and ever the Great Father who was sent to us — gave us the new book of the free souls (?) ...

. . . .

Strive, you Hearers, increasingly add more piety so that you too shall come to the resting place of the gods and become joyful in the New Paradise. — Kulamagāyadn.[62]

. . . .

Blessed be the shepherd, the judge, the well-ruling one (?), the leader, the powerful one, the life. Blessed be the eternal dominion, the fortunate divine lord of the strong, the permanent world-ruler of the brave chieftains; to the throne of the righteous sovereign of the pure intelligent powerful apostles we pay homage. We bend our knee, we sing to your glory, God Narisaf, Sovereign of the Light.

. . . .

... you are ... eternal realm. Lead me ... to my own family. Fortunate (?) every man who in purity and truth recognizes, O God, your skill, manliness and miraculous power. I will take pains and be patient; I will keep zeal by day and by night in order to complete, O God, your advice and order. Worldly pleasure and the things of the world, that Āz (Greed) has prepared with activity and much trickery, I have abandoned at your advice. Hear, oh God, my praise and quickly receive my worship and my prayer. Lead me up from this poisonous depth! This is the road, this is the secret, this is the great commandment and the gate of salvation. Fulfil, oh God, your will in me! May your glory protect me and always increase my patience, zeal and fear (of God), My eye, ear ...".

[M 39, Parthian: *MM* III: 883-86; *Cat*, p. 4]

The pleasure of the world and the lust of appearance, and the things of the world are like unto sweet food mixed with poison: Hold back your soul from their trap! The beings that are deluded through the religions, are terrified. They find no going

out (i.e., salvation) ... and wisdom they do not know. Through
blind habits they perish. Their nature has been turned into
eternal bondage and ruin for them. They fall into hell after
hell, from which they will not again find any way out (and)
in which there is no peace or wellbeing. For us, Elect and
Hearers, joy has been prepared, the palace, the throne and the
garland for ever and ever. Even the Hearers become immortal.
Have mercy, Beneficent God, on me, the grateful ... the
smallest one of (your) sons and the faithful one; for I pray night
and day. Lead my soul to the Eternal Paradise!

Your Light I will give praise, Second Greatness, God Narisaf.
Lovely apparition, brilliance ... judge and witness of all ...
thousand-eyed great Light ... wise [63], where you sat down ...
and the Light ... . [With you lives the Mother] of the Righteous;
near you is also the Living Spirit; (near you are) the mighty
Fathers who gather pearls, the light leaders of the two great
Lamps. There is a spring of peace where the gods dwell. They
move the world and shine out splendor. Entirely full of joy
(are) the divine dwelling places, the noble ships, the spiritual
vessels. The overwhelming Powers, the giants, battle-stirrers,
take away the Light from all creatures. They (i.e., the emanations of the Third Messenger) seduce the demons of wrath
by the two forms (sc. male and female) of the Light. They go
and come as (in) evident joy of heart, of their own will, [in]
miraculous power. The chariots of Light are the gate to the
realm (of God), glad (is) the song that sounds from them. You,
God Narisaf, I will praise; reverence first to you with all (your)
greatness. In mercy save also me, a child! Louder I will bless
you, the one with the sweet name, the saviour ... the leader,
the judge, save my soul! You, Mani with the dear name, I will
praise, I, [the son of] Mar Mani with the sweet name; [save]
my soul! — My soul and self I will ... to you, oh God, ...

[M 77, Parthian: *MM* III: 886-88; cf. M. Schwartz, *JRAS*, 1966, p. 120;
Cat. p. 7]

O just and friendly God *(bag)*, provident Deity *(yazd)*, help me
and you yourself be my support. You are blessed, Illuminator,
God Mihr,[64] great Light. You are the brilliance and the
splendor of the seven climes of the world. Your light shines

in every land and region. Your spirit-course is faster than thought, swifter than the wind moves, more rapid than the night at eve. Your sight is splendid, full of splendor then (?) (your) white sign, lofty your beautiful banner which all the saved follow. The seven climes of the whole world have been arranged, according to the course of the judge, in East, West, North, and South. Above in the sky the 12 gates have been opened each with leaves two by two, three by three having one region each (?). The zone is exactly divided into 12 districts and lands, (with) their marches and frontiers, according to the course of the illuminator. The wise helmsman passes on high through those six thresholds, he shines light upon earth through those 12 gates: 360 dwellings with gates towards one side, 360 dwellings with gates towards the other side. In those 30 revolutions the palaces have been separately prepared, the 12 hours and straight and curved (?) paths. Separately the forms appeared: frontier, [march, la]nd, threshold, gate, revolution, hour, and dwelling. When first the illuminator shone, his course was in the North; for also the First Man had come to the battle-field from there. The world, where he himself is, there there will be six hours (double hours ?): three afterwards and three before, so that the day there becomes two-winged (?) ... he always runs from the North to the East, from the East to the South and from the South to the West. With zeal he swiftly runs, one ...[65]

[M 67 R II, 12 to end, Parthian: *MM* III: 888-90; *Cat.* p. 7]

... the Great Sovereign (i.e., here, the Third Messenger) becomes ...; and by his visible appearance all lands are convulsed; for it opens the fastenings. And in all lands there is great terror, and the Life[66] that is locked up in all productions, gets liberation and purification, and ...

. . . .

That powerful Light escaped and went out; and all these Powers that saw that form were charmed; for they had not before seen that beauty and praised form from the Living Family (i.e., the Light Gods); and neither had they such ...

[From M 1003, Middle Persian: Ed. W. Sundermann, lines 158-169 and 207-217; *Cat.* p. 63]

... the Light of this Righteous God that is God Narisah himself, the Sovereign of the (two) Light chariots (i.e., the sun and moon), the vivifier, the physician and the saviour ...

[T II D 77 I = M 5532 R, Middle Persian, with one Parthian word *(wxd)*: *MM* I: 192, n. 6; *Cat.* p. 110]

In a hymn addressed to the Father of Light, who is "hidden", as he in no way is concerned with the world where his emanations, his *signs* or *aspects*, operate on his behalf, the Third Messenger is the Beautiful East:

You are praised and living, wakeful and eternal. Your sign, your Self, your aspect is our beneficent Father, the Beautiful East, (who is) the form and appearance, the aspect and power of the Father, the first ancestor, the hidden and miraculous giant.

[M 679 V, 8-15, Parthian: W.B. Henning, "Bráhman," *TPS*, 1944, pp. 112-13; *Cat.* p. 46]

The Light is come, and near the leader. Arise, brethren, give praise!
Abandon (?) sleep, awake, behold the Light which is drawn near.
He has come to the world!
All the sons of Darkness hide.
The Light is come, and near the dawn! Arise, brethren, give praise!
We shall forget the dark night.
The sign of the lofty realm has become apparent; and all who have eyes, perceive.
Spirits, souls and all creatures look upon him and arise from (their) fall.
He gives health and joy to the world ... he takes away fear ...
All the demons, wild beasts and vermin are afraid; they depart afar off from him ...
... and he puts and end to pain.

[Select lines from M 30, Parthian: Mary Boyce, "On Mithra in the Manichaean Pantheon," *A Locust's Leg : Studies in honour of S.H. Taqizadeh*, ed. W.B. Henning and Ehsan Yarshater (London, 1962), pp. 50-51; *Cat.* p. 4]

ABBREVIATIONS

AM	*Asia Major*, London.
AOH	*Acta Orientalia Hungarica*, Budapest.
APAW	*Abhandlungen der Königlich Preussischen Akademie der Wissenschaften*, Berlin.
ArOr	*Archiv Orientální*, Prague.
BBB	W. Henning, *Ein manichäisches Bet- und Beichtbuch*. *APAW* 1936. Berlin 1937.
BSO(A)S	*Bulletin of the School of Oriental (and African) Studies*, London.
Cat.	Mary Boyce, *A Catalogue of the Iranian Manuscripts in Manichean Script in the German Turfan Collection*. *Deutsche Akademie der Wissenschaften zu Berlin. Institut für Orientforschung*. Veröffentlichung Nr. 45, Berlin 1960.
CSCO	*Corpus Scriptorum Christianorum Orientalium*. Paris-Louvain.
HR II	F.W.K. Müller, *Handschriften-Reste in Estrangelo-Schrift aus Turfan, Chinesisch-Turkistan*, II. *Aus dem Anhang zu den APAW aus dem Jahre* 1904.
JA	*Journal Asiatique*, Paris
JAOS	*Journal of the American Oriental Society*.
JRAS	*Journal of the Royal Asiatic Society*.
MIO	*Mitteilungen des Instituts für Orientforschung*, Berlin.
MM I-III	F.C. Andreas - W. Henning, *Mitteliranische Manichaica aus Chinesisch-Turkestan* I-III, *SPAW* 1932, 1933, 1934.
NGWG	*Nachrichten von der Gesellschaft der Wissenschaften zu Göttingen*.
PG	Migne's *Patrologia Graeca*.
RÉA	*Revue des études arméniennes*, Paris.

SHAW   *Sitzungsberichte der Heidelberger Akademie der Wissenschaften.*

SPAW   *Sitzungsberichte der Königlich Preussischen Akademie der Wissenschaften,* Berlin.

TPS   *Transactions of the Philological Society,* London.

W.-L. I   E. Waldschmidt — W. Lentz, *Die Stellung Jesu im Manichäismus. APAW* 1926, Nr. 4.

W.-L. II   E. Waldschmidt — W. Lentz, *Manichäische Dogmatik aus chinesischen und iranischen Texten. SPAW* 1933.

ZII   *Zeitschrift für Indologie und Iranistik.*

The texts referred to as "Ed. W. Sundermann" and here translated from the manuscript by kind permission of author and publisher have now appeared in Werner Sundermann, *Mittelpersische und parthische kosmogonische und Parabeltexte der Manichäer mit einigen Bemerkungen zu Motiven der Parabeltexte von Friedmar Geissler.* Schriften zur Geschichte und Kultur des Alten Orients. 8. Berliner Turfantexte IV. Akademie der Wissenschaften der DDR (Berlin, 1973).

NOTES

1. On the dates of Mani, see G. Haloun and W. B. Henning, "The Compendium of the Doctrines and Styles of the Teaching of Mani, the Buddha of Light," *AM*, n.s. 3 (1952): 196-201, and as to this — a diverging concept — S. H. Taqizadeh: "The Dates of Mani's Life," ibid. 6 (1957): 106-15.

2. There can be no doubt that the inscription zndyky (line 10 at the beginning) really stands for Manichaeans. Sprengling's text: *Third Century Iran* (Chicago, 1953), p. 47. As to the concept zandik, see H. H. Schaeder, *Iranische Beiträge*, vol. 1 (Halle, 1930).

3. The Parthian Fragment T. II D 163 (M 6031), line 11, Henning, *BSOS* 10: 948.

4. *Gujastak Abalish*, ed. A. Barthelemy (Paris, 1887), p. 31.

5. *De mathematicis, maleficis et Manichaeis*, in A. Adam, *Texte zum Manichäismus* (Berlin, 1954), pp. 82-83.

6. Ed. Aug. Brinkmann (Leipzig, 1895).

7. Edition of Ch. H. Beeson (Leipzig, 1906). The problem of who the author may be is, incidentally, quite obscure. As to the influence of *Acta Archelai* upon posterity, cf. Henri-Charles Puech, *Le Manichéisme* (Paris, 1949), p. 99, n. 10.

8. A. Rücker, *Des Heiligen Ephräm des Syrers Hymnen gegen die Irrlehren* (Munich, 1928), p. 4.

9. Published by R. P. Casey (Harvard Theological Studies, no. 15 [1931]). Cf. p. 16 ff.

10. Athanasius, *Vita Antonii*, Migne PG 26, 957. 15. Cf. *Vita* 20.

11. Ed. Chavannes et P. Pelliot, "Un Traité Manichéen Retrouvé en Chine," *JA*, 1911, p. 501.

12. Ed. P. de Lagarde, *Titi Bostreni quae ex opere contra Manichaeos edito in codice Hamburrgensi servata sunt graece* and *Titi Bostreni contra Manichaeos libri quatuor syriace*. (Both editions Leipzig, 1859.)

13. As to Augustine's anti-Manichaean treatises, see Prosper Alfaric, *Les Ecritures Manichéennes*, vol. 1 (Paris, 1918), p. 115.

14. Alfaric (ibid., p. 111 f.) gives a short reference to the most important Christian and Islamic treatises against Manichaeism through the centuries.

15. In two vols. (Amsterdam, 1734-39).

16. W. B. Henning, "The Book of the Giants, "*BSOAS* 11 (1943): 52.

17. The complete edition (ed. G. Flügel, J. Roediger, and A. Müller) appeared in 1871-72.

18. *Chronologie orientalischer Völker von Albērūnī* (Leipzig, 1878; English edition, 1879).

19. *Mani : Forschungen über die manichäische Religion*, vol. 1 (Berlin, 1889). (Vol. 2 never appeared.)

20. *Inscriptions mandaïtes des coupes de Khouabir* (Paris, 1898). Text also *CSCO*, script. syr. ser. 2, vol. 66 ed. Scher. Detailed treatment by F. Cumont, "La cosmogonie manichéenne d'après Théodore bar Khôni," in *Recherches sur le manichéisme*, vol. 1. (Brussels, 1908), pp. 1-80, and by A. V. Williams Jackson in *Researches in Manichaeism* (New York, 1932), pp. 221-54. See also p. 255 f.

21. "Handschriftenreste in Estrangeloschrift aus Turfan," *SPAW*, 1904, pp. 348-52.

22. *SPAW*, 1932, 1933, 1934. Here should also be mentioned W. B. Henning, "Ein manishäisches Bet- und Beichtbuch," *APAW*, 1936.

23. *Manis Zeit und Leben* (Prague, 1962).

24. *Mani and Manichaeism* (London, 1965).

25. On the work on the Coptic Manichaica, see A. Böhlig, "Die Arbeit an den Koptischen Manichaica," in *Mysterion und Wahrheit: Gesammelte Beiträge zur spätantiken Religionsgeschichte* (Leiden, 1968), p. 177 ff.

26. A. Henrichs and L. Koenen "Ein griechischer Mani-Codex," *Zeitschrift für Papyrologie und Epigraphik* vol. 5, no. 2 (1970): 97 ff. See also R. Köbert, "Orientalistische Bemerkungen zum Kölner Mani-Codex," and L. Koenen "Das Datum der Offenbarung und Geburt Manis," *Zeitschrift für Papyrologie und Epigraphik*, vol. 8, no. 3 (1971): 243-50, Richard N. Frye, "The Cologne Greek Codex about Mani," *Ex Orbe Religionum: Studia Geo Widengren oblata*, vol. 1 (Leiden, 1972): 424-29, and Albert Henrichs. Mani and the Babylonian Baptists: A Historical Confrontation, *Harvard Studies in Classical Philology* vol. 77 (1973): 23 ff.

27. On the history of research see H.S. Nyberg, "Forschungen über den Manichäismus," *ZNW* 34 (1935): 453 ff., and J. Ries, "Introduction aux études manichéennes. Quatre siècles de recherches," *Ephemerides Theologicae Lovanienses* 33 (1957): 453-82, and 35 (1959): 362-409 (=*Analecta Lovaniensia Biblica et Orientalia*, ser. 3, nos. 7 (1957) and 11 (1959). For an almost full bibliography (to about 1965) see Jes P. Asmussen, *Xᵘāstvānīft: Studies in Manichaeism* (Copenhagen, 1965), p. 265 ff.

28. One of Ahrmēn's demons that as a deserter told secrets to Ohrmizd and, according to the Armenian Eznik from Kolb (fifth century, the only other witness mentioning Mahmi) thus demonstrated the latter's ridiculous powerlessness, in the eyes of the Manichaeans, in *their* interpretation of the rôle of Ohrmizd, a gross example of blasphemy!

29. According to others letters indicating a certain number of converts, but the more detailed Sogdian version of the same text relates the activity of a *man* by that name.

30. Provincial capital on the road from Ktesiphon to Hamadan.

31. I.e., the duties of the Hearers towards the Elect (food, clothes, etc.).

32. What follows is a late legend on the missionary activity in the East, an aethiological legend trying to show, anachronistically, the old age and originality (a product of Mar Ammō) of the eastern branch of the Manichaean Church, the *Dēnāvariyya*.

33. To assemble the gates = to prevent the senses from letting in worldly and fatal impressions and thoughts.

34. In Middle Persian, Sogdian, Chinese, and Turkish texts this word is used about the Column of Glory.

35. The old Syriac translation has retained the final consonant (qlylg, dmng), cf. Friedrich Schulthess, *Kalila und Dimna. Syrisch und deutsch* II (Berlin 1911), p. 172, Arabic *Kalîla wa Dimna*, like New Persian (cf. Rumi, *Mathnawi* IV, 2203: *dar kalīla*) and Latin (*Kelila, Kalila, Kalile, Dimna, Dimne*).

36. Latest edition: Johann von Capua, *Beispiele der alten Weisen. Altindische Erzählungen in lateinischer und deutscher Übersetzung*, ed. Friedmar Geissler (Berlin, D.D.R.: Deutsche Akademie der Wissenschaften zu Berlin, Institut für Orientforschung, Veröffentlichung, no. 52, Berlin, 1960).

37. *The Panchatantra*, ed. Johannes Hertel, Harvard Oriental Series, vol. 11 (Cambridge, Mass., 1908), pp. 269-70, *Das Pañcatantram (Textus ornatior). Eine altindische Märchensammlung*. Zum ersten Male übersetzt von Richard Schmidt (Leipzig s.a.), pp. 295-96. In the Sanskrit version the lucky fish is a frog.

38. Official and writer at the Byzantine court of the sixth century (Justinian I). His principal work is a general history of his own age. The quotations here given are from his *Anékdota*, 22: 25, a *chronique scandaleuse* that still puzzles scholars.

39. Pali *yakkha*, a demon, a supernatural being attendant — in Hinduism and Buddhism — on Vaishravana (Kuvera), the guardian of the north. They appear now as inoffensive, now as imps of evil.

40. Goblins or evil spirits, but not all equally bad; see John Dowson, *A Classical Dictionary of Hindu Mythology and Religion, Geography, History, and Literature*, 8th ed. (London, 1953), p. 254 f.

41. Kardêr (Kartir) was a great and zealous Zoroastrian priest and, so to say, the real founder of orthodoxy under the early Sasanids. He took great effort in driving Buddhists, Christians, Manichaeans, etc., out of the Empire. His deeds he made known, with immense, but probably just self-confidence, in several Middle Persian inscriptions: One on the *Ka'bah* of Zarathustra, another at Naqsh-i Rustam, a third at Naqsh-i Rajab (here: "And I Kartir am most eminent in rectitude in the Empire"), and a fourth at Sar Mashhad south of Kazerun. Different from him is the Kartir son of Ardavān mentioned above. See Richard N. Frye, *The Heritage of Persia* (London, 1962), pp. 218 ff.; idem., "The Middle Persian Inscription of Kartīr at Naqš-i Rajab," *Indo-Iranian Journal* 8 (1965): 211 ff.; Marie-Louise Chaumont, "L'inscription de Kartīr à la 'Ka'bah de Zoroastre'," *JA*, 1960, pp. 33·80; and Philippe Gignoux, "L'inscription de Kartir à Sar Mašhad," *JA*, 1968, pp. 387-418.

42. In the cosmography of Hinduism, Jainism, and Buddhism, the mountain of the gods in the middle of the world. A Buddhist text in Khotanese identifies this mountain with the Iranian mythical *Harā-bərəz-* (Harburz, Alburz) known from Zoroastrian books. See H.W. Bailey, *Indo-Scythian Studies Being Khotanese Texts*, vol. 2 (Cambridge. 1953), p. VII.

43. The Bema feast itself is discussed in detail by C.R.C. Allberry, "Das manichäische Bema-Fest," *Zeitschrift für die neutestamentliche Wissenschaft* 37 (1938): 2-10 and *Journal of Theological Studies*, 1938, p. 344 f.

44. The divinized cry (of the Living Spirit) and answer (of Ohrmizd, the First Man).

45. See H.H. Schaeder, "Iranica," *AGWG*, 1934, p. 74.

46. Parthian, *HR* II: 109; *Cat.*, p. 3.

47. See W.B. Henning, "The Murder of the Magi," *JRAS*, 1944, p. 137 ff.

48. The common Iranian word for demon. The word is a loanword in the Armenian *(dew)*, where however its meaning is strongly coloured by Christian ideas, cf. Fr. Macler, *Les dew arméniens, Petite Bibliothèque Arménienne*, vol. 12 (Paris, 1929), p. 24.

49. See W.B. Henning, "Das Verbum des Mittelpersischen der Turfanfragmente, *ZII* 9 (1933): 224.

50. *BSOAS* 11 (1943): 179.

51. The coming savior in Buddhism, used about Mani.

52. Maybe the Four Gospels; Gospel = Wind in e.g., the Christian Bishop Irenaeus of Lyons, second century.

53. The three parts of the Old Testament?

54. W. Bang und A. von Gabain, "Ein uigurisches Fragment über den manichäeischen Windgott," *Ungarische Jahrbücher* 8, p. 248 ff.

55. The cry and the answer are divinized and come to play a great part in Manichaean theology.

56. Legatus primus is Ohrmizd, Legatus secundus, the Living Spirit.

57. Loan-word from the Greek *(speira)*. On this word and a word of the same orthography but of a different meaning, see Otakar Klíma, "Two Comments to the Middle Iranian Lexicon," *Dr. J.M. Unvala Memorial Volume* (Bombay, 1964), pp. 35-36.

58. See Martin Schwartz, "Iranian **draw-* 'to lead astray'," *JRAS*, 1966, p. 120.

59. Cf. Otakar Klíma, "Beiträge zum mittelpersischen Lexikon," *ArOr* 37 (1969); 546 ff.

60. See A. V. Williams Jackson, "The Doctrine of the Bolos in Manichaean Eschatology," *JAOS* 58: 225-34.

61. See A.J. van Windekens, "Études iraniennes et tokhariennes," *Le Muséon* 62 (1949): 128.

62. Author's name or the name of the person to whom the hymn is dedicated.

63. See A.J. van Windekens, op. cit., p. 127.

64. In Middle Persian texts God Mihr (Mihryazd) = the Living Spirit.

65. On Manichaean astronomy, see Walter Henning, "Ein manichäisches Henochbuch," *SPAW*, 1934, p. 32 ff.

66. Middle Persian plural to indicate the presence of Life (i.e., Light), in *many* places.